Stones into Schools

ALSO BY GREG MORTENSON

Three Cups of Tea
ONE MAN'S MISSION TO PROMOTE PEACE . . . ONE SCHOOL AT A TIME
(WITH DAVID OLIVER RELIN)

Three Cups of Tea
ONE MAN'S JOURNEY TO CHANGE THE WORLD . . . ONE CHILD AT A TIME
(THE YOUNG READERS EDITION, WITH DAVID OLIVER RELIN,
ADAPTED BY SARAH THOMSON)

Listen to the Wind
THE STORY OF DR. GREG AND THREE CUPS OF TEA
(WITH SUSAN L. ROTH, ILLUSTRATIONS BY SUSAN L. ROTH)

Stones into Schools

PROMOTING PEACE WITH BOOKS, NOT BOMBS,
IN AFGHANISTAN AND PAKISTAN

GREG MORTENSON

Viking

VIKING
Published by the Penguin Group
Penguin Group (USA) Inc., 375 Hudson Street,
New York, New York 10014, U.S.A.
Penguin Group (Canada), 90 Eglinton Avenue East, Suite 700, Toronto, Ontario,
Canada M4P 2Y3 (a division of Pearson Penguin Canada Inc.)
Penguin Books Ltd, 80 Strand, London WC2R 0RL, England
Penguin Ireland, 25 St. Stephen's Green, Dublin 2, Ireland
(a division of Penguin Books Ltd)
Penguin Books Australia Ltd, 250 Camberwell Road, Camberwell, Victoria 3124,
Australia(a division of Pearson Australia Group Pty Ltd)
Penguin Books India Pvt Ltd, 11 Community Centre, Panchsheel Park,New Delhi – 110 017, India
Penguin Group (NZ), 67 Apollo Drive, Rosedale, North Shore 0632,
New Zealand (a division of Pearson New Zealand Ltd)
Penguin Books (South Africa) (Pty) Ltd, 24 Sturdee Avenue,
Rosebank, Johannesburg 2196, South Africa

Penguin Books Ltd, Registered Offices: 80 Strand, London WC2R 0RL, England

First published in 2009 by Viking Penguin, a member of Penguin Group (USA) Inc.

1 3 5 7 9 10 8 6 4 2

Copyright © Greg Mortenson, 2009
Foreword copyright © Khaled Hosseini, 2009
All rights reserved

Portions of this book originally appeared in slightly different form as "No Bachcheh Left Behind"
by Kevin Fedarko, Outside magazine. Copyright © Kevin Fedarko, 2008.

Map illustrations by Jim McMahon (pages viii–xi) and Jeffrey L. Ward (pages xii–xiii)

LIBRARY OF CONGRESS CATALOGING-IN-PUBLICATION DATA
Mortenson, Greg.
Stones into schools : promoting peace with books, not bombs, in Afghanistan and
Pakistan / Greg Mortenson.
p. cm.
Includes index.
ISBN 978-0-670-02115-4
ISBN 978-0-670-02158-1 (export edition)
1. Girls' schools—Afghanistan.   2. Girls' schools—Pakistan.   3. Humanitarian
assistance, American—Afghanistan.   4. Humanitarian assistance, American—Pakistan.
5. Peace-building—Afghanistan.   6. Peace-building—Pakistan.   7. Mortenson, Greg—Anecdotes.
8. Taliban—History.   I. Title.
LC2330.M66 2006
371.823'4209581—dc22   2009030812

Printed in the United States of America
Set in Stemple Garamond
Designed by Elke Sigal

*To the noble people of Afghanistan and Pakistan
and to the 120 million school-age children in the world
who are deprived of their right of education*

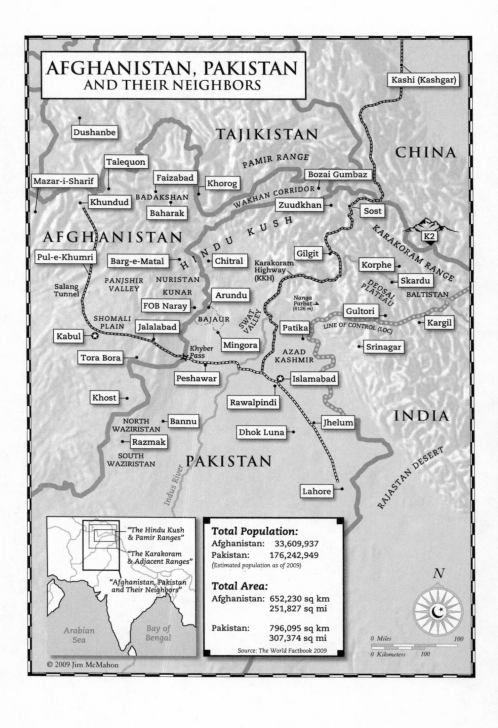

AFGHANISTAN, PAKISTAN
AND THEIR NEIGHBORS

Kashi (Kashgar)

TAJIKISTAN

CHINA

Dushanbe

PAMIR RANGE

Talequon

Faizabad

Khorog

Bozai Gumbaz

Mazar-i-Sharif

BADAKSHAN

WAKHAN CORRIDOR

Zuudkhan

Sost

Khundud

Baharak

K2

AFGHANISTAN

HINDU KUSH

KARAKORAM RANGE

Pul-e-Khumri

Barg-e-Matal

Chitral

Gilgit

Korphe

Karakoram
Highway
(KKH)

Skardu

Salang
Tunnel

PANJSHIR
VALLEY

NURISTAN

DEOSAI
PLATEAU

BALTISTAN

KUNAR

Arundu

Nanga
Parbat
(8126 m)

Gultori

FOB Naray

Kargil

SHOMALI
PLAIN

BAJAUR

SWAT
VALLEY

Patika

LINE OF CONTROL (LOC)

Kabul

Jalalabad

Mingora

Srinagar

Tora Bora

Khyber
Pass

AZAD
KASHMIR

Peshawar

Islamabad

INDIA

Khost

Rawalpindi

Jhelum

NORTH
WAZIRISTAN

Bannu

Dhok Luna

Razmak

SOUTH
WAZIRISTAN

PAKISTAN

RAJASTAN DESERT

Indus River

Lahore

"The Hindu Kush
& Pamir Ranges"

"The Karakoram
& Adjacent Ranges"

"Afghanistan, Pakistan
and Their Neighbors"

Arabian
Sea

Bay of
Bengal

© 2009 Jim McMahon

Total Population:
Afghanistan: 33,609,937
Pakistan: 176,242,949
(Estimated population as of 2009)

Total Area:
Afghanistan: 652,230 sq km
              251,827 sq mi

Pakistan: 796,095 sq km
              307,374 sq mi

Source: The World Factbook 2009

N

0 Miles   100

0 Kilometers   100

CENTRAL ASIA INSTITUTE
SCHOOLS CIRCA OCTOBER 2009

TAJIKISTAN

CHINA

PAMIR RANGE

Faizabad

WAKHAN CORRIDOR

12 2

Khundud
BADAKSHAN
TAKHAR
9 1

7 1 1
CHARPURSON
VALLEY

AFGHANISTAN

1
2
HUNZA
VALLEY

5
ISHKOMEN
VALLEY

HINDU KUSH

Karakoram
Highway
(KKH)

KARAKORAM RANGE

K2

Salang
Tunnel

4
PANJSHIR
VALLEY

NORTHWEST
FRONTIER
PROVINCE

NURISTAN

11
KUNAR

BRALDU
VALLEY

3

7

SHEGAR
VALLEY

2

3
THALLE
VALLEY

9 1
HUSHE
VALLEY

BALTISTAN

3 1
SHOMALI
PLAIN

Kabul

BAJAUR

SWAT VALLEY

GULTORI
VALLEY

2

21 1 2
INDIS
VALLEY

Jalalabad

1

1
1
WARDAK

Khyber
Pass

1

1
17
NEEUM
VALLEY

LINE OF CONTROL (LOC)

1
UROZGAN

KHOST

3

Peshawar

1

AZAD
KASHMIR

Islamabad

1
Rawalpindi

INDIA

NORTH
WAZIRISTAN

JHEUM
VALLEY

2
2

SOUTH
WAZIRISTAN

PAKISTAN

Indus River

PUNJAB

Lahore

RAJASTAN DESERT

Mian Channu
1

N

School Legend:

● Primary/Middle School

▲ High School

◆ Other School:
(Medical, English,
Computer, Model, etc.)

Note: Numerals in symbols
denote number of CAI
schools in that region

0 Miles   100

0 Kilometers   100

© 2009 Jim McMahon

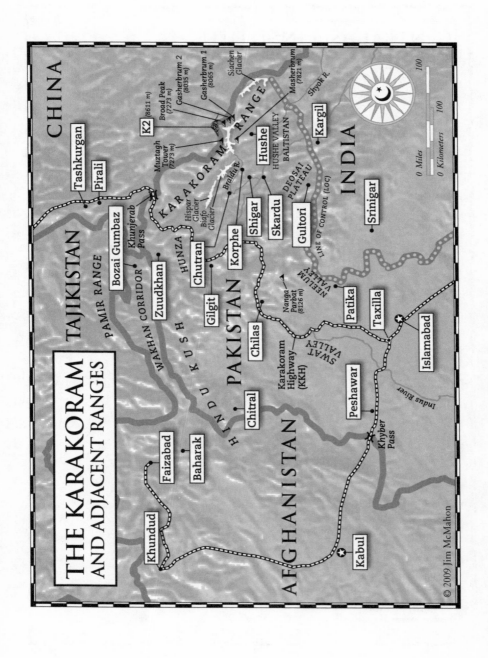

THE KARAKORAM AND ADJACENT RANGES

CHINA

TAJIKISTAN

PAMIR RANGE

Tashkurgan

Pirali

Bozai Gumbaz

Khunjerab Pass

Zuudkhan

WAKHAN CORRIDOR

HUNZA

Gilgit

Chutran

Korphe

Braldu R.

Biafo Glacier

Hispar Glacier

KARAKORAM RANGE

Muztagh Tower (7273 m)

K2 (8611 m)

Broad Peak (7273 m)

Gasherbrum 2 (8035 m)

Gasherbrum 1 (8065 m)

Siachen Glacier

Masherbrum (7821 m)

Shyok R.

Kargil

Hushe

HUSHE VALLEY

BALTISTAN

Shigar

Skardu

DEOSAI PLATEAU

Gultori

LINE OF CONTROL (LOC)

Srinigar

INDIA

NEELUM VALLEY

Nanga Parbat (8126 m)

HINDU KUSH

Chitral

Faizabad

Baharak

Khundud

Chilas

Karakoram Highway (KKH)

SWAT VALLEY

Peshawar

Khyber Pass

Kabul

AFGHANISTAN

PAKISTAN

Patika

Taxilla

Islamabad

Indus River

100

100

0 Miles

0 Kilometers

© 2009 Jim McMahon

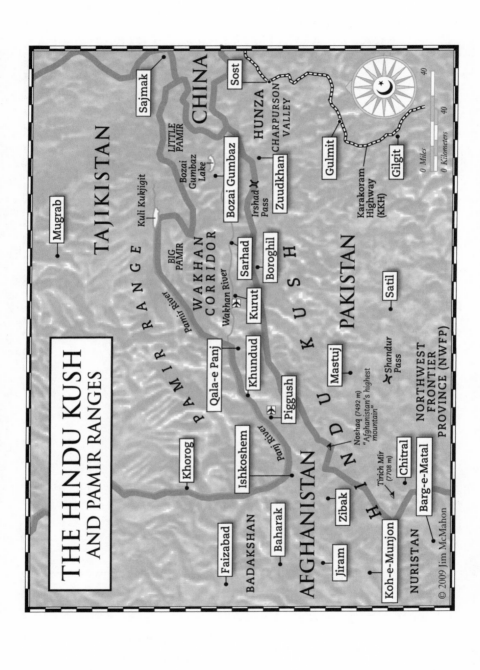

THE HINDU KUSH
AND PAMIR RANGES

TAJIKISTAN

CHINA

Mugrab

Sajmak

Kuli Kukjigit

LITTLE
PAMIR

Bozai
Gumbaz
Lake

Sost

HUNZA

CHARPURSON
VALLEY

Bozai Gumbaz

BIG
PAMIR

P A M I R   R A N G E

WAKHAN CORRIDOR

Pamir River

Sarhad

Irshad
Pass

Zuudkhan

Boroghil

Gulmit

Wakhan River

Kurut

Karakoram
Highway
(KKH)

Gilgit

0 Miles   40

0 Kilometers   40

Khorog

Qala-e Panj

Khundud

Piggush

Mastuj

H I N D U   K U S H

PAKISTAN

Satil

Shandur
Pass

Ishkoshem

Panj River

Noshaq (7492 m)
"Afghanistan's highest
mountain"

Faizabad

BADAKSHAN

Baharak

Zibak

Tirich Mir
(7708 m)

Chitral

NORTHWEST
FRONTIER
PROVINCE (NWFP)

Jiram

Koh-e-Munjon

Barg-e-Matal

AFGHANISTAN

NURISTAN

© 2009 Jim McMahon

AFGHANISTAN PROVINCES
& FEDERALLY ADMINISTERED TRIBAL AREAS

TAJIKISTAN

N

Faizabad

WAKHAN

Baharak

Taleqon

BADAKSHAN

Zuudkhan

Ishkoshem

TAKHAR

NORTHERN AREAS

Chitral

PANJSHIR

AFGHANISTAN

NURISTAN

Naray

KUNAR

SWAT VALLEY

Asadabad • BAJAUR

Mingora

LAGHMAN

MOHMAND

NORTHWEST
FRONTIER
PROVINCE
(NWFP)

Kabul

KABUL

Jalalabad

NANGARHAR

Khyber Pass

Mardan

Landi Kotal

LOGAR

KHYBER

Peshawar

AZAD
KASHMIR

Parachinar

PATIKA

ORAKZAI

Attock

INDIA

Islamabad

Gardez

KURRAM

Kohat

KHOST

Khost

PAKISTAN

NORTH
WAZIRISTAN

Miranshah

Bannu

PATIKA

FEDERALLY
ADMINISTERED
TRIBAL AREAS
(FATA)

PUNJAB

AFGHANISTAN: 34 provinces

PAKISTAN: 4 provinces and
Federally Administered Tribal Areas

SOUTH
WAZIRISTAN

Wana

Tank

| 0 Miles | 50 | 100 |

| 0 Kilometers 50 | 100 |

© 2009 Jeffrey L. Ward

ETHNIC DISTRIBUTION
WITHIN PAKISTAN AND AFGHANISTAN

UZBEKISTAN   TAJIKISTAN   CHINA

TURKMENISTAN

N

Faizabad

Sheberghan •   Mazar-i-Sharif •   • Khundud   Gilgit

Panjsher   Skardu
Valley

NWFP

Bahmiyan •   • Jalalabad   • Mardan

Herat •   ★ Kabul   • Peshawar   ★ Islamabad

Khost •   • Rawalpindi

Farah •   • Tarin Kowt   FATA   • Jhelum

AFGHANISTAN   PUNJAB

• Kandahar   • Lahore

IRAN

PAKISTAN

• Quetta

• Chaggi

0 Miles   100   200   BALOCHISTAN   INDIA

0 Kilometers   200

ETHNOLINGUISTIC GROUPS

Pashtun	Wakhi	Baloch/Sindhi
Tajik	Kirghiz	Sindhi
Hazara	Turkmen	Punjabi
Uzbek	Nuristani	Burushuski
Aimak	Baloch	Balti
Kalash	Kashmiri	Mixed/other

TOTAL POPULATION (2008)

AFGHANISTAN: *32 million*
PAKISTAN: *173 million*

PERCENTAGE OF TOTAL POPULATION

AFGHANISTAN	PAKISTAN
Pashtun 42%	*Punjabi 44%*
Tajik 27%	*Pashtun 15%*
Hazara 9%	*Sindhi 14%*
Uzbek 8%	*Baloch 4%*
Other 14%	*Other 23%*

© 2009 Jeffrey L. Ward

Who's Who

Ali, Haji: Greg Mortenson's first mentor and chief of Korphe village, Pakistan; passed away in 2001

Ali, Jahan: Granddaughter of Haji Ali and Central Asia Institute's first female student to graduate from high school

Ali, Niaz: Spiritual leader of the Kirghiz in the Wakhan, Afghanistan

Ali, Twaha: Haji Ali's son and father of Jahan; from Korphe, Pakistan

Al-Zawahiri, Ayman: Egyptian physician; second in command of Al Qaeda

Baig, Faisal: Wakhi elder from Charpurson Valley, Pakistan, and the CAI's security manager

Baig, Nasreen: CAI student from Charpurson Valley who is now studying to be a maternal health-care worker

Baig, Saidullah: The CAI's manager in Charpurson Valley, Pakistan

bin Laden, Osama: Saudi Arabian leader of Al Qaeda who is now either in hiding or dead

Bishop, Tara: Greg Mortenson's wife and a psychotherapist

Boi, Tashi: Village chief of Sarhad, in the Wakhan Corridor, Afghanistan

Chabot, Doug: Climber, avalanche expert, and CAI volunteer

Chabot, Genevieve: CAI scholarship program manager; married to Doug Chabot

Chaudry, Shaukat Ali: Former Taliban member, now a teacher in the CAI girls' school in Azad Kashmir, Pakistan

Dostum, General Rashid: Uzbek ethnic leader based in Mazar-i-Sharif, Afghanistan

Ghani, Dr. Ashraf: Former minister of education of Afghanistan

Gulmarjan: CAI Afghan student killed by a land mine in 2003 at the age of twelve

Hoerni, Dr. Jean: Silicon transistor pioneer and cofounder of CAI with Greg Mortenson; passed away in 1997

Hosseini, Khaled: Physician, philanthropist, and best-selling author of *The Kite Runner* and *A Thousand Splendid Suns*

Hussain, Aziza: First maternal health-care worker in Charpurson Valley, Pakistan

Ibrahim, Haji Mohammed: *Shura* (elder) leader from Uruzgan Province, Afghanistan

Karimi, Wakil: CAI manager for Afghanistan

Karzai, Hamid: President of Afghanistan

Khan, Abdul Rashid: *Amir* (leader) of the Kirghiz people in the Wakhan Corridor, Afghanistan

Khan, Sadhar: Tajik leader in Badakshan who was CAI's first supporter in the region

Khan, Sarfraz: CAI's remote areas project manager; from Pakistan

Khan, Shah Ismael: *Pir* (leader) of the Wakhi people in Afghanistan

Khan, Wohid: Badakshan border security commander in Afghanistan

Kolenda, Colonel Christopher: Former commander of Forward Operating Base (FOB) Naray and currently a key U.S. military strategist in Afghanistan

Kosar, Parveen: The first female high school graduate in the Wakhan, and now a maternal health-care worker there

Leitinger, Christiane: Director of Pennies for Peace

McChrystal, Major General Stanley: Commander of ISAF (and U.S.) military forces in Afghanistan; proponent of counterinsurgency methodology

Massoud, Ahmed Shah: Tajik military commander called the Lion of the Panjshir for his role in driving out the Soviets; assassinated by al Qaeda on September 9, 2001

Minhas, Suleman: CAI's Punjab Province manager, based in Islamabad; formerly a taxi driver

Mirza, Colonel Ilyas: Retired Pakistani military aviation officer and general manager of Askari Aviation, a civil aviation charter company

Mohammed, Mullah: Former Taliban bookkeeper and CAI accountant for the entire Wakhan region

Mortenson, Amira and Khyber: Children of Greg Mortenson and Tara Bishop

Mortenson, Christa: Younger sister of Greg Mortenson; passed away in 1992 when she was twenty-three

Mortenson, Irvin "Dempsey" and Jerene: Greg Mortenson's parents

Mughal, Ghosia: CAI student from Azad Kashmir

Mullen, Admiral Mike: Chairman of the U.S. Joint Chiefs of Staff and the military leader who inaugurated a CAI girls' school in Afghanistan in July 2009. Married to Deborah.

Musharraf, Pervez: President of Pakistan from 1999 to 2008; former Pakistani army chief of staff

Myatt, Major General Mike: Former commander of the Marine Expeditionary Force who led the invasion into Kuwait

Najibullah, Mohammed: Afghanistan's communist leader and former president; killed by the Taliban in 1996

Nicholson, Major Jason: U.S. military officer based at the Pentagon

Olson, Admiral Eric: SOCOM commander of the combined U.S. Special Forces. Admiral Olson and his wife Marilyn are advocates of girls' education and introduced Mortenson to several senior military commanders

Omar, Mullah: Afghan Pashtun tribal leader of the Taliban; thought to be hiding in Quetta, Pakistan

Parvi, Haji Ghulam: CAI's Pakistan-based manager and accountant, who has overseen the establishment of over fifty schools

Petraeus, General David: U.S. CENTCOM commander. It was from his wife, Holly, that General Petraeus first learned about *Three Cups of Tea.*

Rahman, Abdullah: Former medical librarian and CAI driver in Afghanistan

Razak, Abdul: Former expedition cook from Baltistan; eldest CAI employee; also known as Apo (old man)

Sen, Amartya: 1998 winner of the Nobel Prize in economics

Shabir, Saida: Headmistress of Gundi Piran girls' school in Pattika, Azad Kashmir, Pakistan, which was destroyed by the 2005 earthquake

Shah, Zahir: King of Afghanistan who fled to Italy in 1973 and returned to Afghanistan after 9/11, remaining there until his death in 2007

Shaheen, Farzana: CAI student in Azad Kashmir, Pakistan

Sipes, Jennifer: CAI's operations manager in Montana

Contents

PART III
The School on the Roof of the World

Foreword

by
KHALED HOSSEINI

The muddled war in Afghanistan is now in its eighth year, and has become the most urgent foreign policy challenge facing President Obama. Against a backdrop of rising conflict, respected think tanks like the Atlantic Council have published reports calling Afghanistan a failing state. The country indeed faces enormous problems: a violent, spiraling insurgency that is hampering the rule of law and developmental efforts, the growth of record crops of poppies, extreme poverty, criminality, homelessness, joblessness, lack of access to clean water, continuing problems with the status of women, and a central government that has struggled to protect its people and provide basic services.

But there are success stories as well in post-9/11 Afghanistan, and the most meaningful of them is education. If we accept the premise that education is the key to achieving positive, long-lasting change in Afghanistan, then it is impossible to overstate how encouraging it is that this year nearly eight and a half million children will attend school in Afghanistan, with girls accounting for nearly 40 percent of enrollment.

No one understands this better than Greg Mortenson, the founder of 131 schools in Afghanistan and Pakistan that provide education to nearly 58,000 students. No one grasps better the profound impact and ripple effect of even one child's education. And, arguably, no single individual or organization has done more to advance the American cause in Afghanistan than Greg Mortenson, a courteous, soft-spoken man who with his genial smile and warm handshake has shown the U.S. military how the so-called battle for the hearts and minds is fought. And how it is won.

Greg's philosophy is not complicated. He believes quite sincerely that the conflict in Afghanistan will ultimately not be won with guns and air strikes, but with books, notebooks, and pencils, the tools of socioeconomic well-being. To deprive Afghan children of education, he tells us, is to bankrupt the future of the country, and doom any prospects of Afghanistan becoming someday a more prosperous and productive state. Despite fatwas issued against him, despite threats from the Taliban and other extremists, he has done everything he can to make sure that this does not happen.

Very crucially, he has spearheaded efforts to educate girls and young women. Not an easy task in a region where parents routinely keep their daughters out of school and where long-standing cultural traditions have deprived women of the right to education. But in village after village, Greg has reached out to religious leaders and elders to help convince parents to send their girls to school. This is because Greg believes, as I do, that if Afghanistan has any chance to become a more prosperous nation, it will require the full engagement of its women as part of the process. And for that to happen, women have to be given access to schools, and their education has to be one of the cornerstones of national reconstruction and development. As he says repeatedly, mantralike, "If you educate a boy, you educate an individual, but if you educate a girl, you educate a community."

Lastly, Greg has done all this with charm, grace, patience, and unfailing humility. He has listened carefully, built relationships with village leaders based on trust and respect, and involved people in shaping their own future. He has taken the time to learn the local culture—courtesy, hospitality, respect for elders—and to understand and appreciate the role Islam plays in people's daily lives. No wonder the U.S. military has recruited Greg as a consultant on how to fashion better relationships with tribal leaders and village elders. They have a lot to learn from him. We all do.

Tashakor, Greg jan, for all you do.

KHALED HOSSEINI

www.khaledhosseinifoundation.org
Author of the international best sellers
The Kite Runner and *A Thousand Splendid Suns*

Stones into Schools

Introduction

Every leaf of the tree becomes a page of the Book
Once the heart is opened and it has learnt to read
—SAADI OF SHIRAZ

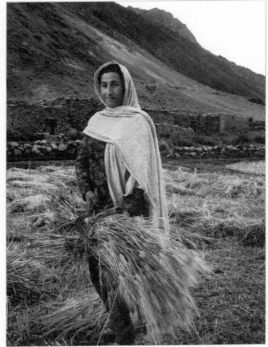

Nasreen at home in Zuudkhan village, Pakistan

*I*n September of 2008, a woman with piercing green eyes named Nasreen Baig embarked on an arduous journey from her home in the tiny Pakistani village of Zuudkhan south along the Indus River and down the precipitous Karakoram Highway to the bustling city of Rawalpindi. The three-day trip—first on foot, then on horseback, and later by jeep and bus—took Nasreen, her husband, and their three small children from the sparsely populated Charpurson Valley, in the extreme northern part of Pakistan, directly into the heart of the Punjab, home to more than eighty-five million people. With the exception of a few farming tools, most of their worldly possessions, including a Koran, were crammed into a black suitcase that was cinched together with baling twine. They also carried a bulging burlap sack whose contents—every stitch of spare clothing they weren't wearing on their backs—were as jumbled and mixed up as the pieces of Nasreen's own story.

In 1984, at the age of five, Nasreen started attending one of the first coeducational schools to open up in the north of Pakistan, a region where women were traditionally denied the opportunity to learn reading and writing. Excelling at her classes, she distinguished herself as one of the smartest students in the school until 1992, when her mother unexpectedly died of pneumonia and Nasreen was forced to abandon her studies in order to care for her blind father, Sultan Mehmood, and her four siblings. Eventually her father remarried, and Nasreen's new stepmother, a woman who believed that girls had no business pursuing education, would taunt Nasreen late at night when she tried to continue her studies by the light of a kerosene lantern. "Women should work instead of reading books," her stepmother would rail. "Books will poison your mind and you will become a worthless wife and mother!"

Nasreen didn't see it that way. During her school years, she had acquired a rather bold dream for someone with resources as limited as hers: She had resolved that one day she would become a maternal health-care provider—a profession she had first been exposed to when roving government health-care teams would make their annual rounds through the local villages. She vividly remembers the joy with which she anticipated immunization shots, just so she could interact with the workers in their white cloaks. "My favorite smell was the antiseptic they would use," she says. "Also, I envied how they would write down all the babies' names, heights and weights, and immunization details in tidy rows in a spiral notebook."

Fueled by her dream, Nasreen studied relentlessly, despite her stepmother's harassment. "After tending to my brothers and sisters and doing all the household work," she recalls, "I would wait till everyone was asleep, and then late at night I would read." She persisted in this manner until 1995 when, at the age of fifteen, she received her metric diploma—the equivalent of a high-school degree—becoming one of the first of a handful of women from northern Pakistan's Hunza region ever to do so. As the brightest student and one of the first female graduates for miles around, she was now poised to make good on her ambition.

In 1999, Nasreen was offered an annual scholarship of $1,200 by our nonprofit Central Asia Institute, a stipend that would pay her tuition, room, and board for a two-year course of study and enable her to obtain her rural medical assistant degree. With these qualifications, Nasreen could then carry her skills north over a treacherous 16,335-foot pass into the Wakhan Corridor—a remote portion of Afghanistan just a few miles north of Zuudkhan where Nasreen's ancestors originally came from and where more women die each year during childbirth than anywhere else on earth.

By this point, however, Nasreen had been betrothed to a handsome but lazy young man from a nearby village, and her mother-in-law, Bibi Nissa, feared that Nasreen's scholarship would rob her household of the new daughter-in-law's labor. Even though there were no other qualified girls in the Charpurson Valley to replace Nasreen as a scholarship candidate, Zuudkhan's *tanzeem*—the council of elders who decide all matters of local importance—upheld Bibi Nissa's objections and forbade Nasreen from accepting her stipend, thereby consigning her to a life of near slavery that remains the destiny of so many promising young women in the remote villages of Pakistan and Afghanistan.

During the ten years that followed this decision, Nasreen toiled twelve- to sixteen-hour days tending goats and sheep in the mountains, tilling her family's potato fields, hauling water in metal jerricans, and gathering up eighty-pound bags of firewood and moist patties of yak dung—Zuudkhan's two primary sources of heating fuel during the six-month-long winters. During this time she also gave birth to three babies and suffered two miscarriages, all without the attendance of a maternal health-care worker.

Despite the drudgery and the frustration, Nasreen patiently waited out her decade of servitude. What's more, during her brief moments of respite, she kept her health-care dream alive by seeking out and caring for the sick, the elderly, and the dying within her community. "The lamp in my life refused to be snuffed out," she says. "God never let the kerosene of hope run dry."

Then, in the summer of 2007, the leadership of Zuudkhan's *tanzeem* changed and the elders decided to set aside their opposition. Nasreen spent a year in the town of Gilgit attending a preparatory school to build back her academic skills after the long hiatus. Finally, in the summer of 2008, with her scholarship in hand, Nasreen was free to travel to Rawalpindi to resume her studies.

Today, Nasreen is a year away from completing her medical training program, but she has decided to continue with her schooling in order to complete a full OB-GYN nursing degree. Sometime in 2012, she hopes to move her family to the Wakhan and begin providing the kind of medical care that this region, one of the most isolated and forbidding places on earth, so desperately needs. As for her "lost years," Nasreen harbors no bitterness whatsoever, mainly because she is convinced that her experiences imparted some essential insights.

"Allah taught me the lesson of patience while also giving me the tools to truly understand what it means to live in poverty," she says. "I do not regret the wait."

During the exact same time that Nasreen and her family were making their way down the Karakoram Highway toward Rawalpindi, I was paying a visit of my own to a small town in the heart of the Rocky Mountains. This was no different from any of the other 120-odd trips I make each year to cities across the United States and abroad in order to promote educational opportunities for women like Nasreen throughout Pakistan and Afghanistan. By the rather warped standards of my own schedule, September 18, 2008, was a fairly ordinary day. During the preceding week, I had given seventeen speeches at schools, churches, and libraries in nine other cities; and at three o'clock the following morning, I was slated to board a private plane that would take me from Durango to my next appearance, a children's peace rally in Rockford, Illinois. This would be followed by another eighteen lectures in eight more cities before returning to Pakistan on October 6. Somewhere in the middle of this, I was also hoping desperately for a one-day reprieve with my family.

In many other respects, however, September 18 was anything but ordinary. The previous weekend the federal government had permitted the investment firm Lehman Brothers to go bankrupt before attempting an $85 billion–dollar rescue of the insurance giant AIG. By the time the stock market had closed that afternoon, the Dow Jones was in free fall and the entire U.S. financial system seemed to be hovering on the brink of collapse. In short, I could not possibly have selected a worse time to stand in front of a group of Americans and ask them to pull out their checkbooks.

Fortunately, perhaps, my schedule allowed no time to contemplate the absurdity of this. It was a few minutes before 7:00 P.M. when, having already completed six back-to-back lectures, I dashed across the campus of Fort Lewis College to the gym, where more than four thousand people—almost a third of the town—had formed an impossibly long line. The fire marshal would eventually be forced to bar the door and prevent the final three hundred of these folks from entering the building. (Someone later told me that Durango hadn't seen a crowd this size since Willie Nelson last came to town.)

Although the talks I give in these kinds of settings tend to vary according to the composition of my audience, I always begin with the same words: *As-Salaam Alaaikum*—the Islamic invocation that means "May peace be upon you." And regardless of where I wind up steering the discussion, the heart of my presentation always includes the story of a promise.

This story begins in Pakistan in 1993, the year I attempted to climb K2, the world's second-highest mountain, only to be forced to turn back two thousand feet shy of the summit. After making my way back to K2 base camp, I then got lost while trekking down the thirty-nine-mile Baltoro Glacier and wound up staggering into a little village called Korphe (pronounced "KOR-fay"), a place so destitute that one in every three children perished before the age of one. It was in Korphe that I was provided with shelter, food, tea, and a bed. And it was in Korphe one afternoon during my recuperation that I stumbled across eighty-two children sitting outside writing their lessons with sticks in the dirt, with no teacher in sight. One of those young students was a girl named Chocho, and somehow she got me to promise the community that I would someday return and build them a school.

The fulfillment of that promise involves a tale that recounts my fumbling efforts in Berkeley, where I worked as a nurse, to sell my car, my climbing gear, and all of my books in order to raise the necessary money—and the subsequent chain of events through which a lost mountaineer eventually came to discover his life's calling by fostering education and literacy in the impoverished Muslim villages of the western Himalayas.

A few years ago, I put these events together into a book called *Three Cups of Tea*, and as those who have read all 338 pages can attest, it's a rather long and unusual story. It is also a story that has always struck me as the chronicle of an ordinary man who inadvertently bumbled into an extraordinary place.

When it really comes down to it, I am nothing more than a fellow who took a wrong turn in the mountains and never quite managed to find his way home. My initial vision, if you could call it that, involved helping a village knock together a 2,218-square-foot schoolhouse without any plumbing or electricity in the middle of a barley field at 10,400 feet. In a world filled with bold dreamers and big ideas, it's hard to imagine a goal more humble than this. And it is the diminutive stature of this beginning that may help to explain why I now live my days beset by an almost continuous sense of wonderment and confusion.

Although I have, by my staff's estimate, completed a total of 680 appearances in more than 270 cities and towns from Miami and Los Angeles to Anchorage and Shreveport over the last three years, each time I travel somewhere new, I am still shocked by the sheer number of people who flock to hear this tale. Last summer in Boston, when the organizers of a talk I was giving at Northeastern University realized how many people wanted to learn about our schools in Pakistan and Afghanistan, they booked me into a hockey stadium and filled the place with 5,600 people. A week later at a basketball arena in Murfreesboro, Tennessee, 9,500 folks showed up and my speech had to be broadcast on a Jumbotron.

That's a big change for someone who once considered himself lucky to get the attention of half a dozen bored shoppers at a Patagonia or REI outlet, and perhaps the only thing that amazes me more than the size of these audiences is their dedication and interest. It is not unusual for people to drive six or even twelve hours to hear these presentations, then stand in line for another two hours simply to get their books autographed. But perhaps the most noteworthy testament to their commitment is the sort of thing that took place on that September night in Durango.

On the very same evening that Ben Bernanke, the chairman of the Federal Reserve, was informing members of the House Financial Services Committee that the entire global economy was days away from a complete meltdown, the citizens of Durango, population 16,007, presented the Central Asia Institute with checks totaling nearly $125,000. A single contribution of $50,000 was given by George Boedecker, the founder of the shoe manufacturer Crocs. But the rest of the money came from the sort of individuals who will never know what it means to own a brand or run a corporation. Ranchers, housewives, and salesclerks. Mechanics, teachers, and plumbers. Secretaries, dental hygienists, students, and retirees. People who embody the virtues, as well as the limitations, of a life that is fashioned from humble materials. People, in other words, as ordinary and as unremarkable as me and you.

In my view, that is amazing enough all by itself, but then consider this.

Very few of the people in Durango that night had ever been to Pakistan or Afghanistan. No more than a handful could have been Muslim. And it was doubtful that a single one would ever see, with his own eyes, the schools, books, pencils, and teacher salaries that his money would pay for. Still, they opened their hearts and gave. There, on the threshold of the greatest economic collapse since the Great Depression, in the midst of an era when so many of our leaders have encouraged us to subordinate our noblest impulses to our basest fears, a small community in Colorado responded in exactly the same way as every other city and town to which I have traveled in America since this whole saga got started.

"When you hand this money over to the folks over there on the other side of the world," said one local businessman, who had tears in his eyes as he spoke, "just tell them that it comes from a little town in the mountains of Colorado so that their daughters can go to school."

Here, then, is the source of my wonder and confusion. Why do so many Americans seem to care so deeply about people who live in a place that is so far away? Despite everything that has happened, how can our anger and our fear be transcended so consistently by our decency? And what is it about the promise of educating children—especially girls—that so often, and with such fervor, seems to evoke what is best in all of us?

In addition to being a profoundly bewildered man, I am an incorrigible introvert. I am awkward, soft-spoken, ineloquent, and intensely shy. I do not enjoy speaking in public, posing for photographs, or asking other people for money. I dream of privacy, I revere silence, and I loathe any action that involves drawing attention to myself. (Even creating these pages was painful: It took a supreme effort on the part of both my wife, Tara, and my editor, Paul Slovak, to force me to agree to write it in the first person—an approach that is emphatically *not* my cup of tea.) In the Christmas pageant of life, the characters I admire most—and the only roles for which I would ever consider auditioning— are the ox and the donkey.

Given these facts, the duties of speaking, promoting, and fund-raising into which I have been thrust during the last several years have often made me feel like a man caught in the act of conducting an illicit affair with the dark side of his own personality. For politicians and celebrities, a lifestyle that entails an endless schmoozefest of back slapping and elbow rubbing seems to come as instinctively (and as necessarily) as breathing. I, on the other hand, find this kind of thing extremely discomforting—partly because it sits so directly at odds with my deepest instincts about personal decorum, and partly because it so often leaves me wrestling with a sense of shame. All of which may help to explain why the unexpected and runaway success of *Three Cups of Tea* seems, at least in my view, to be charged with such a wicked irony.

As I write this in the summer of 2009, the book is currently logging its 130th week on the *New York Times* best-seller list for trade paperback nonfiction, has sold more than three million copies, and is being published in three dozen countries. As you might imagine, this has produced the kind of publicity and attention that I find intolerable. But it has also opened the door to some extraordinary opportunities.

Hard currency goes a long way in the impoverished hinterlands of the western Himalayas, where $20 is enough to educate a first grader for an entire year, $340 can send a girl to four years of high school on a full-ride scholarship, and $50,000 is sufficient to build and outfit an eight-room schoolhouse and endow the teachers' salaries for the first five years. During the four years since *Three Cups of Tea* was first published, our contributors have not only financed the construction of scores of new school buildings but have also funded scholarships, teacher-training programs, and women's vocational centers in remote villages extending from the glacier-carved valleys of the Karakoram to the wind-blasted reaches north of the Hindu Kush. Every bit as important as these projects, however, is the awareness that our donors have helped to raise about the vital importance of girls' education.

Studies from the World Bank indicate that just *one* year of primary school can result in an income bump of 10 percent to 20 percent for women later in life. According to Yale economist Paul T. Schultz, an extra year of secondary school may raise that same girl's lifetime wages by an additional 15 to 25 percent. And the effects don't end there. A number of studies indicate that in communities where a majority of the girls are educated through the fifth grade, infant mortality drops significantly after a single generation. At the same time—and somewhat paradoxically— basic education for girls correlates perfectly with lower, more sustainable population growth. In communities where girls have received more education, they marry later and have fewer children than their illiterate counterparts.

These premises, which I also encountered in the work of

Nobel Prize–winning economist Amartya Sen, are now accepted by many development experts around the world. (The definitive short book on the general subject is *What Works in Girls' Education: Evidence and Policies from the Developing World,* by Barbara Herz and Gene B. Sperling.) Simply put, young women are the single biggest potential agents of change in the developing world—a phenomenon that is sometimes referred to as the Girl Effect and that echoes an African proverb I often heard during my childhood years in Tanzania: "If you teach a boy, you educate an individual; but if you teach a girl, you educate a community." No other factor even comes close to matching the cascade of positive changes triggered by teaching a single girl how to read and write. In military parlance, girls' education is a "force multiplier"—and in impoverished Muslim societies, the ripple effects of female literacy can be profound.

Take the issue that many in the West would consider to be the most pressing of all. "Jihad" is an Arabic word referring to a "struggle" that is undertaken as a means of perfecting oneself, improving society, or defeating the perceived enemies of Islam. In Muslim societies, a person who has been manipulated into believing in extremist violence or terrorism often seeks the permission of his mother before he may join a militant jihad—and educated women, as a rule, tend to withhold their blessing for such things. Following 9/11, for example, the Taliban's forces suffered from significantly increased desertions; as a countermeasure, they began targeting their recruitment efforts on regions where female literacy was especially low.

Education, of course, offers no guarantee that a mother will refuse to endorse violent jihad, but it certainly helps to stack the odds against the men—and, yes, they are invariably men—who promote the lie that killing innocent people is in keeping with the teachings of the Koran. Although I am not an authority on the Koran, religious scholars have repeatedly emphasized to me during the last sixteen years that murder and suicide are two of the most unforgivable sins in Islam.

It is important to be clear about the fact that the aim of the Central Asia Institute is not indoctrination. We have no agenda other than assisting rural women with their two most frequent requests: "We don't want our babies to die, and we want our children to go to school." And in the process of addressing those wishes, it is certainly not our aim to teach the children of Pakistan and Afghanistan to think or to act like Americans. We simply want them to have the chance to attend schools that offer a balanced, nonextremist education. In this respect, we're also extremely sensitive to the difference between literacy and ideology. It is our belief that the first helps to thwart intolerance, challenge dogma, and reinforce our common humanity. The second does the opposite.

At the moment, female literacy in rural Afghanistan continues to languish in the single digits. In rural Pakistan, the figures are a little higher, but not by much. The demand for schools, teachers, books, desks, notebooks, uniforms, chalkboards, paper, and pencils in these two Islamic nations is immense, and the benefits of American investment in this "intellectual infrastructure" are indisputably clear. Nothing that has happened since my unsuccessful attempt to climb K2—including 9/11—has changed my conviction that promoting female literacy represents the best way forward for Pakistan and for Afghanistan.

Education is one of the many basic values that Americans of all faiths share with Muslim people everywhere.

When journalists write about the achievements of the Central Asia Institute, they often tend to trot out the same sets of figures. They are fond of mentioning that during the sixteen years since my failure as a K2 climber, I have completed thirty-nine trips to Pakistan and Afghanistan, where, without using a dollar of money from the U.S. government, the Central Asia Institute has established 131 schools that currently serve more than 58,000 students, most of them girls. These articles also claim that the response to my "message" cuts across the lines that traditionally divide politics, religion, and class in the United States. They point out that the fans of *Three Cups of Tea* include not only Bill Clinton, Laura and Barbara Bush, John Kerry, and Colin Powell, but also prominent military leaders such as CENTCOM commander General David Petraeus, chairman of the Joint Chiefs of Staff Admiral Mike Mullen, and SOCOM (Special Forces) commander Admiral Eric Olson. To my honor, *Three Cups of Tea* is now required reading for all officers enrolled in counterinsurgency courses at the Pentagon.

In some ways, these tidbits of information may be useful—if nothing else, they convey a general sense of what we've been up to and what others think of our work. On a personal level, however, this approach tends to miss the point. If there is a metric by which I measure the achievements of the Central Asia Institute, it is not the amount of donations we receive each year, or the number of people who have read *Three Cups of Tea,* or even the number of schools we have built. In fact, it really has nothing to do with math and everything to do with the girls whose lives have been changed through education. In the end, the thing I care most about—the flame that burns at the center of my work, the heat around which I cup my hands—are their stories.

And by God's grace, what marvelous stories these women can tell.

Take the case of Jahan Ali, whose grandfather, Haji Ali, was Korphe's *nurmadhar* (village chief) and who became my most important mentor. On the first day I met Jahan in September of 1993, she extracted a promise from me that if she graduated, we would send her off to a maternal health-care program—an IOU that she triumphantly collected on nine years later. After finishing grad school in Korphe, she went on to enroll in advanced studies in public policy administration. Meanwhile, back home, Jahan's father has been trying to marry her off—she is currently twenty-three years old, and her bride-price, thanks to her education, has now shot from five to fifty adult rams. Jahan, however, declares that she first intends to become a community leader and a member of Pakistan's parliament. "I am not going to get married until I achieve my goal," she recently told me. "*Inshallah* (God willing), someday I will become a super-lady."

Then there is the story of Shakila Khan, who graduated with the first class at our school in Hushe, a village in a valley to the south of Korphe that sits in the shadow of Masherbrum, one of the highest mountains on earth. Currently in her third year at Fatima Memorial Hospital in Lahore and scoring in the nineties, Shakila is slated to become the first locally educated female physician ever to emerge from Baltistan's population of 300,000 people. She is currently twenty-two years old and intends to return to the Hushe Valley to work among her people. "My main two goals," she says, "are that I do not want women to die in childbirth or babies to die in their first year."

Finally, consider Aziza Hussain, who grew up in the Hunza Valley, not far from the point where the Karhuram Highway crosses into China. After graduating from Gulmit Federal Government Girls' High School in 1997 and completing a two-year maternal health-care program on a CAI scholarship, Aziza, too, insisted on returning home to ply her skills within her own community—a place where as many as twenty women perished each year during childbirth. Since Aziza came back in 2000, not a single woman in the area has died giving birth.

Thirteen years after we completed our first school in Korphe, the maiden generation of Central Asia Institute women have graduated and are preparing to launch their careers. These women are now making "first ascents" far more dramatic and impressive than the achievements of western climbers, such as myself, who have been coming into these mountains ever since Aleister Crowley, the British poet, spy, and yogic devotee, made the first attempt to climb K2 in 1902.

Already, these daughters have climbed so much higher than we mountaineers ever dared to dream.

Serious and worthy efforts to promote schooling for girls are currently taking place all over the world, from Guatemala and Egypt to Bangladesh and Uganda. The unusual twist that the Central Asia Institute applies to this enterprise, however, is encapsulated in the title of *Three Cups of Tea*, which refers to a Balti saying that Haji Ali invoked during one of my first visits to his village. "The first cup of tea you share with us, you are a stranger," he intoned. "The second cup, you are a friend. But with the third cup, you become family—and for our families we are willing to do anything, even die."

Of the many lessons that that old man imparted to me, this was perhaps the greatest. It underscores the paramount importance of taking the time to build relationships, while simultaneously affirming the basic truth that in order to get things done in this part of the world, it is essential to listen with humility to what others have to say. The solution to every problem, Haji Ali firmly believed, begins with drinking tea. And so it has proven.

After my first encounter with Haji Ali in 1993, I returned to the United States, raised twelve thousand dollars, and then went back a year later to Pakistan, where I purchased a massive load of cement, lumber, and other supplies in the city of Rawalpindi. This material was piled onto a Bedford truck and ferried up the Karakoram Highway to the town of Skardu, a trip that took three days. There it was transferred to jeeps and driven to the end of the road, eighteen miles from Korphe—where I arrived with the expectation of being greeted like a hero. Instead, I was informed (after drinking several cups of tea with Haji Ali) that before we could start construction on the school, we had to build a bridge. The reason? It would be impossible to ferry the construction materials over the roaring Braldu inside the only device spanning the river, a rickety wooden basket suspended beneath a 350-foot cable.

Perhaps I should have thought of this earlier; in any case, the unexpected turn of events seemed like a disaster. It forced me to retreat back to the United States, where I had to convince my main benefactor, Dr. Jean Hoerni, to contribute even *more* money, which was then used to purchase even *more* construction materials and transport these supplies to the edge of the Braldu, where the residents of Korphe built a 282-foot-long suspension bridge over the river. In the end, the whole exercise set the project back nearly two years.

At the time, I found this detour and its delays utterly maddening. Only years later did I begin to appreciate the enormous symbolic significance of the fact that before building a school, it was imperative to build a bridge. The school, of course, would house all of the hopes that are raised by the promise of education. But the bridge represented something more elemental: the relationships upon which those hopes would be sustained over time—and without which any promise would amount to little more than empty words.

Korphe's schoolhouse was finished in December 1996, and since then each and every school we have built has been preceded by a bridge. Not necessarily a physical structure, but a span of emotional links that are forged over many years and many shared cups of tea.

This philosophy means that some of our projects can grind along at a pace that mirrors the ponderous movement of the

Karakoram glaciers. For example, in Chunda, a conservative rural village in Baltistan, it took *eight years* for us to convince the local mullah, an immensely cautious and pious man, to permit a single girl to attend school. Today, however, more than three hundred girls study in Chunda—and we take great pride in the fact that they do so with the full support of the very same mullah who once stood in their way. His change of heart affirms the notion that good relationships often demand titanic patience.

Like Nasreen Baig, the green-eyed nurse from the Charpurson, we do not regret the wait. As any wise village elder will tell you, anything truly important is worth doing very, *very* slowly.

The book that you are holding in your hands picks up where *Three Cups of Tea* left off in 2003 and is partly a chronicle of how that process has continued to unfold in Pakistan during the last several years. Mostly, however, this new book traces our efforts to take our work into a whole new region, the remote northeastern corner of Afghanistan. It is a place that has proved even more challenging than Pakistan, and the saga of what my staff sometimes calls our "Afghan adventure" is framed loosely in the context of a single school.

If *Three Cups of Tea* lays out the narrative of our first school—the seed with which we started our planting—then this is the tale of the most remote of all our projects, the flower in the farthest corner of the garden. No project has ever taken us so long or required such complex logistics as the little school we built next to the old Kirghiz burial grounds in the heart of the Afghan Pamir's *Bam-I-Dunya*, the "Rooftop of the World." And next to Korphe itself, no school is closer to my heart, because, in ways both large and small, it was the most miraculous. It arose out of a promise made in 1999 during an unlikely meeting that seemed lifted from the pages of a novel set in the thirteenth century, when the horsemen of Genghis Khan roamed the steppes of central Asia. And it drew us into the land of the Afghans, the only place that has ever threatened to usurp the affection and the love I harbor for Pakistan.

Part of what has made this school such a surprise is that so many other urgent projects were demanding our attention during the ten years it took to make good on our promise. The fact that we refused to let it go, even amid an earthquake in Kashmir in 2005 and other challenges that are recounted in the pages that follow, is a testament less to me than to the vision and the persistence of the Central Asia Institute's staff, and in particular to a group of twelve men whom I affectionately call the Dirty Dozen. If there are any heroes here, it is they; and for the most part this book is their story, because without these men, none of it would have happened. If the daughters who flock to our schools represent the fire we've lit, then these men are the fuel that sustains the flames. They have guided, pushed, and inspired me in more ways than I can recount, and their commitment and sacrifices run so deep that whatever we achieve will ultimately belong not to me but to them. Without their example and their resourcefulness, I would still be nothing more than a dirtbag mountaineer subsisting on ramen noodles and living in the back of his car.

As you'll see, the story of the little gem of a school that we built in the most remote corner of central Asia is a roundabout tale—a thread that like the twisting roads we ply in our battered Land Cruiser through the passes of the Karakoram and the Hindu Kush can sometimes get lost amid the unexpected detours and the landslide of complications that cascade down upon anyone who ventures into that harsh and wondrous part of the world. But these digressions and dead ends may also provide something that readers of *Three Cups of Tea* have been requesting from me for years. What they've wanted, more than anything else, is a window into the day-to-day mechanics and rhythms of the Central Asia Institute. A sense of what it feels like to lay the physical and emotional foundation for girls' education, book by book and brick by brick, in the middle of Taliban country. If nothing else, this new work should fulfill that request.

I should also note that the first part of this story will cover some ground that may already be familiar to readers of *Three Cups of Tea*. I thought this was necessary and important because several of these early events began to shape themselves into a meaningful pattern only over time. Back when they took place, I did not understand the full significance of these experiences and lessons they imparted, nor did I realize where they fit into the larger story that it is my privilege to tell here.

In short, it was only after having moved forward a considerable distance that I was fully able to comprehend where we had been—a phenomenon that would not have surprised Haji Ali, who, to my sadness, passed away in 2001. Haji Ali never learned to read or write, and over the course of seven decades he left his home village only once, to perform a pilgrimage to Mecca. Nevertheless, he understood that hope resides in the future, while perspective and wisdom are almost always found by looking to the past.

Sometimes, it seems like everything I've ever learned traces back to that irascible old man I first met in the barley fields of Korphe.

GREG MORTENSON
Baharak, Afghanistan
August 2009

PART I

The Promise

Prologue

The education and empowerment of women
throughout the world cannot fail to result in a more caring,
tolerant, just and peaceful life for all.
—AUNG SAN SUU KYI

Greg Mortenson in the Wakhan

*T*he Irshad Pass is one of three great gaps leading north through the Hindu Kush into the most forgotten corner of Afghanistan. Along the crest of this pass the ground is free of snow for only four months each year, and the air is so thin that the traders who employ this route have been known to slice open the nostrils of their donkeys to help them breathe. Beyond the Pakistani high point, the track makes a long, talus-littered descent, at the bottom of which is a massive ravine that forces the trail to perform a sharp dogleg. This means that anyone waiting at the southern entrance to the Irshad cannot see who is coming through the pass until the very last minute—and that is how I came to miss the moment when the squadron of Kirghiz horsemen made their entrance into Pakistan in October of 1999.

It was the keen-eyed Sarfraz Khan—the hunter of the ibex, the ex-commando with the crippled hand—who spotted them first, just as they rounded the corner, from half a mile away. The second he caught sight of them, he leaped up from the blanket on which we were sitting, dashed over to our jeep, flung open the door, and started laying his fist into the horn.

"They are coming, they are coming!" he clamored in Wakhi, unable to contain his excitement. "*Wazdey, Wazdey!* Well done!"

I was about to take another swallow of the *nemek choi* (salt tea) that we had been sipping all morning to ward off the wind and the sleet, but my hand halted when the cup was halfway to my lips, then returned the cup to the ground and gently placed it there while I watched the horsemen advance.

It was not a spectacle one could witness in an offhand manner.

There were fourteen riders, coming fast through a scrim of cold rain, and even from the distance of nearly a thousand yards, the timeworn music of their cavalry—the hollow clomping of the hoofbeats and the metallic clanking of steel in the horses' mouths—cleaved the alpine air. We could hear, too, the muffled creak of wet leather under strain, and a faint patter as thick clods of dirt thrown up by the horses' hooves arced above the riders' heads and rained onto the ground behind them.

The man in the lead was clad in a weather-beaten duster, black leather boots that rose to his knees, and corduroy pants that were dark and shiny with the smear of mutton grease. A battered British Lee Enfield rifle flopped along his back, his waist was belted with a strap of leather so wide that it spanned his belly, and on his head he wore a Soviet-era pile cap whose earflaps galloped with the movement of his horse. The men who followed him carried AK-47s and an abundance of other weapons, and their cartridge belts were slung heavily across their shoulders and chests. Their horses, like his, were short legged and shaggy and iridescent with sweat.

They thundered toward us in a headlong rush until, at the last possible second, they pulled to an abrupt halt and leaped in unison from their saddles with a catlike grace that seemed both cavalier and precise. It was the kind of careless perfection that only men who have spent their entire lives on horseback can achieve.

The leader, I could see now, was a young man with an ill-trimmed mustache and a flat, coppery, wind-burnished face. He was thin and ragged and hardened, and this combination of features made him seem to step directly from a stream of time that flowed unbroken from the forty or fifty generations of his nomadic forbears, who were among the greatest horsemen the world has ever known. Standing there in the mud, he reached into his coat pocket, removed a wad of moist green chewing tobacco, and greeted us with the customary *As-Salaam Alaaikum*. Then he remarked, softly and with great courtesy, that he and his men had been riding for six days without stopping.

They had been dispatched, it turned out, as emissaries from *Commandhan* Abdul Rashid Khan, the leader of the last group of Kirghiz left in the High Pamir. In the impoverished land from which these men had ridden, conditions were now so harsh that each winter their families and their herds of camels, sheep, and yaks seesawed on the threshold of starvation. Yet of all the things that Abdul Rashid's people lacked, what he desired most was the chance for their children to learn to read and write—and therein lay the errand that had drawn this horseman and his retinue over the Irshad Pass.

For the past several years, the horseman explained, strange stories had been filtering into the High Pamir from the southern side the Hindu Kush, tales of a mysterious American mountain climber who was said to be setting up schools in the most remote valleys of northern Pakistan, the places the government didn't seem to care about and where the foreign NGOs refused to venture. There were rumors, too, that in addition to educating the boys, the institutions this man was raising up would also open their doors to any girl who yearned for literacy.

When word had reached Abdul Rashid Khan that the American school builder was scheduled to pay a visit to the Charpurson Valley, he had sent out a platoon of his strongest riders and his swiftest horses to find this man and ask if he would consider coming into Afghanistan to build schools for the sons and the daughters of the Kirghiz.

Few things happen quickly in the hinterlands of the western Himalayas, but there was a special urgency to this man's mission. The first storm of the winter of 1999 was already descending upon the Hindu Kush, and if these horsemen failed to return before the snows blocked the crest of the Irshad, they risked being cut off from their homes and families until the following spring. Preferably right now, but no later than the following morning, they would need to race north over the pass with my answer.

"*Waalaikum-Salaam* (May peace be with you also)," I replied. "I understand that time is short, but first let us go to the home of my friend Sarfraz Khan so that you and your men can eat and take some rest," I told the leader of the horsemen. "Then later, we will talk of Abdul Rashid Khan's request, and we will discuss if it is possible to make a school."

CHAPTER I

The People at the End of the Road

I don't know what your destiny will be, but one thing I know:
the only ones among you who will be really happy
are those who will have sought and found how to serve.
—ALBERT SCHWEITZER

Grand Trunk Highway near Jalalabad, Afghanistan.

Whenever I head for the airport to catch a flight to Pakistan or Afghanistan, my luggage usually includes a small plastic briefcase emblazoned with a green and white bumper sticker that reads THE LAST BEST PLACE. Those words were first put together as the title to an anthology of Montana-based writings that William Kittredge and Annick Smith edited back in 1988. Since then, "The Last Best Place" has become the unofficial motto for the state in which I have spent the last fourteen years living with my wife, Tara, our two children, Amira and Khyber, and our Tibetan terrier, Tashi. The slogan neatly sums up the stirring landscapes and the vast sense of openness that draw so many Americans to Montana, and the words are now as synonymous with my adopted home's identity as the silhouette of the mountains on our license plates.

For me, though, Kittredge's catchphrase carries a radically different meaning.

If you look at the map of the schools that the Central Asia Institute has built since 1995, you will see that nearly every one of our projects is in a location that lacks an educational infrastructure because of geographical isolation, severe poverty, religious extremism, or war. These are areas that few people from the outside world even know about, the regions where almost nobody else goes. They are the places where we begin.

This approach is markedly different from the way development normally works. Most NGOs, for all sorts of sound and well-justified reasons, prefer to establish a base of operations in a region that enjoys favorable access to resources and communications, and only then will these organizations gradually expand into the harder areas. It's a sensible way to proceed. The problem, however, is that if you work in a way that is incremental and controlled, it can sometimes take a lifetime to get to the people who need your help the most. What is far more difficult—and sometimes more dangerous—is to start at the *end* of the road and work your way back. And for better or worse, that's exactly what we do.

The other thing that distinguishes us from some other development groups is that our aim is not to saturate a region with our presence by launching hundreds of projects. We simply want to plant a handful of schools in the hardest places of all, empower the communities in these areas to sustain those projects, and then step back in the hope that the government and other NGOs will start moving toward these points from the areas that aren't quite so rough, until the gap is eventually bridged. Surprisingly often, that's exactly what happens.

In Baltistan, the rugged and beautiful corner of northeastern Pakistan that lies in the heart of the Karakoram, we spent the second half of the 1990s targeting the villages at the farthest ends of the most remote valleys, places at altitudes of up to eleven thousand feet that are perched along the outer limits of human habitation. We broke ground on more than three dozen sturdy, stone-walled schoolhouses, providing construction materials and teachers on the condition that each village chip in free land and labor—and that they agree to increase female enrollment until the girls reached parity with the boys. The first school we established, in Korphe, is in the last human settlement in the Braldu Valley before you reach the Baltoro Glacier, which leads to K2. Our school in Hushe lies at the end of a valley that culminates at the base of Masherbrum, one of the most stunning of the world's great seven-thousand-meter peaks.

In similar fashion, we have also spearheaded projects in areas that are plagued by armed conflict and religious extremism. In 1999, at the request of the Pakistani military, we launched two projects in the Gultori region, where the armies of India and Pakistan were locked in fierce fighting along the contested border of Kashmir. The schools we put in were tucked into the slopes of mountains and featured pitched metal roofs capable of deflecting fallout from the Indian army's artillery shells. More recently, in 2008, we have helped communities in eastern Afghanistan's Kunar Province in building two girls' schools in the center of the volatile border region between Pakistan and Afghanistan that shelters many members of the Taliban. The Pathan tribal leaders who asked for these schools approached us with their initial request for assistance through the commander of an American military base that is located in the same area.

This "last place first" philosophy of ours is unconventional, and it occasionally provokes criticism; but sometimes there is simply no other alternative. If an organization like the CAI doesn't leapfrog directly into such places, another generation or two of girls will have lost the opportunity to attain literacy. In addition to these practical considerations, however, there's another reason why we do things this way—one that has little to do with pragmatism.

The good people who inhabit the frontiers of civilization do not, as a rule, tend to be the world's most sophisticated or cosmopolitan human beings. Often, they aren't especially well educated or refined, nor all that conversant with cutting-edge trends in areas like, say, fashion and current events. Sometimes, they're not even all that friendly. But the folks who live at the end of the road are among the most resilient and the most resourceful human beings you will ever meet. They possess a combination of courage, tenacity, hospitality, and grace that leaves me in awe.

What I have also discovered over the years is that with just a little bit of help, such people are capable of pulling off astonishing things—and in doing so, they sometimes establish a benchmark for the rest of us. When ordinary human beings perform extraordinary acts of generosity, endurance, or compassion, we are all made richer by their example. Like the rivers that flow out of the Karakoram and the Hindu Kush, the inspiration they generate washes down to the rest of us. It waters everyone's fields.

So for me, that THE LAST BEST PLACE sticker on my briefcase doesn't represent a slogan or a marketing campaign to promote the wonders of my home. Instead, those words affirm my belief that the people who live in the last places—the people who are most neglected and least valued by the larger world—often represent the best of who we are and the finest standard of what we are meant to become. This is the power that last places hold over me, and why I have found it impossible to resist their pull.

Back in 1993, when this whole school-building business first got started, the little village of Korphe struck me as the apogee of remoteness, the supreme expression of what it means to live in the very last place at the far end of the road. In the years that followed, it has been my privilege to work in some equally isolated and difficult places that thanks to the people who inhabit them are blessed by the same rough magic as Korphe. But until I met the Kirghiz horsemen who had ridden out of the Wakhan on that October afternoon in 1999, I had never encountered a group of people who came from a place so remote, so austere, that it didn't seem like the end of the road as much as the end of the earth itself.

A place that made even Korphe feel like a suburb of Los Angeles.

The Pashtuns say that when Allah was finished creating the world, he cobbled together all the leftover bits and pieces, and it was from this pile of rubble that he fashioned Afghanistan. The impression of a landscape that has been pieced together from discarded debris is evident in every part of this country, but nowhere is this sense of brokenness more acute than inside the panhandle of northeastern Afghanistan that thrusts between Pakistan and Tajikistan for nearly 120 miles until it touches the border of the People's Republic of China. Some of the loftiest mountain ranges on earth—the Kunlun, the Tien Shan, the Pamirs, the Karakoram, and the Hindu Kush—converge inside or near this region. The highest of their summits soars more than twenty thousand feet, and the inhabitants of the forbidding, desolate, bitterly cold alpine plateaus that stretch beneath those peaks refer to this place as *Bam-I-Dunya*, the "Rooftop of the World."

For more than twenty centuries, the Wakhan Corridor has served as a thoroughfare for traders, diplomats, invading armies, pilgrims, explorers, missionaries, and holy wanderers making their way between central Asia and China. The Corridor not only defined the meeting point between Inner and Outer Tartary—the realms that the Greek geographer Ptolemy called "the Two Scythias"—but also formed one of the most arduous sections of the Silk Road, the four-thousand-mile route by which the civilizations of India, Europe, and the Near East traded and communicated with those of the Far East.

Only a handful of westerners are known to have passed

through the Wakhan, starting with Marco Polo, who spent four years making his way through Persia and across central Asia to reach the court of the Chinese emperor, Kublai Khan. While traversing the length of the Wakhan in 1271, the legendary Venetian traveler wrote of ridgelines so high that birds found it impossible to fly over them and a cold so intense that it stifled the heat of his campfires while robbing the flames of their color. Nearly 350 years later, a Jesuit priest named Benedict de Goes was chosen by his order to follow in Polo's footsteps in search of Cathay. Disguised as an Armenian trader, he joined a caravan of merchants and made his way to the Chinese city of Suchow, where he was detained, became ill, and eventually perished. De Goes's death, in the year 1607, roughly coincided with the Silk Road's final eclipse, as the great terrestrial thoroughfare of trade was supplanted by the sea routes that were being pioneered between Europe and the Far East—although a small but persistent trickle of commerce continued to dribble across the Pamir from Chinese Turkistan to Tibet and Chitral, the northernmost outpost of India.

The Wakhan did not reemerge on the world stage until the later part of the nineteenth century, when Great Britain and Russia began tussling for control of central Asia in the imperial contest known as the Great Game. During this period, Russia was expanding its southern borders toward the ancient cities of the Silk Road, while Britain was seeking to explore and protect the passes through the Himalayas and the Hindu Kush that led to India, the richest gem in Britain's imperial crown. An eccentric collection of explorers and military officers played a cat-and-mouse game along the high country of the Hindu Kush and the Pamirs. In 1895, after the two sides were brought to the brink of war, politicians in London and Saint Petersburg established the Wakhan as a buffer zone to ensure that the underbelly of the czars' kingdom would at no point touch the northernmost crest of the Raj.

Twenty-two years later, the creation of the Soviet Union shut down the Wakhan's northern borders, severing most of the remaining north-south commerce. Then, in 1949, Mao Zedong completed the Communist takeover of China and the Corridor's door to the east was slammed shut, permanently halting almost all east-to-west movement. Within a single generation, a place that had once served as the linchpin of the greatest trade route in history and had later come to demarcate the farthest borders of the world's two foremost imperial powers was transformed into the poorest and the most obscure dead-end road on earth.

Today, the residents of the Corridor are consigned to a state of quarantine that is impossible to imagine for anyone who inhabits a world whose borders are defined by e-mail, Twitter, and satellite phones. Implacably isolated and breathtakingly remote, the Wakhan is central Asia's Ultima Thule: a place so distant and so far beyond the margins of the known world that it seems to delineate not only the outer limits of geography but the edge of civilization itself.

The Kirghiz horsemen who rode over the Irshad Pass in the autumn of 1999 were descendants of nomadic tribes from the Tuva region of Russia who had migrated into central Asia in the thirteenth century, during the rise of the Mongol empire—and for the better part of eight centuries, these tribes' lives revolved around seasonal migrations across the mountain ranges separating what are now eastern Afghanistan, western China, and southern Tajikistan. Each year the tribes would rove freely across the grasslands of the High Pamir with their felt yurts and their flocks of goats, yaks, and double-humped Bactrian camels, unmolested by government officials, tax collectors, or security agents. The winters would be spent in the lower valleys of Tajikistan or western China, where they could shelter from the weather and protect their flocks from bears and wolves. In the summer, they would slowly move back into the alpine grasslands, where the only other inhabitants were Marco Polo sheep, ibex, and other wild animals.

Following the Bolshevik Revolution, the Soviet government devoted much of the 1930s to a policy of forcing the nomadic cultures who inhabited the USSR's central Asian republics to abandon their migratory traditions and settle on collective farms. A group of Kirghiz eventually rebelled against this effort and petitioned the king of Afghanistan for sanctuary in the Wakhan. This protected them from the Soviets, but it reduced their migrations to a series of short shifts between the eastern Wakhan and China's Xinjiang Province. During the 1950s and 1960s, the Chinese Communists restricted these movements even further.

Then in 1978, just prior to the Soviet invasion of Afghanistan, roughly 1,300 Kirghiz led by an imam named Haji Rahman Qul decided to abandon the Pamirs and cross south over the Hindu Kush into Pakistan. They found life in this new home intolerable (the Kirghiz women were forced to follow the rules of purdah, and the heat caused many members of the group to fall ill). After trying unsuccessfully to acquire American visas and move his people to Alaska, Rahman Qul embarked on a new journey in 1982. Referred to as the Last Exodus, this odyssey eventually took his followers to eastern Anatolia, where they were given political asylum by the Turkish government and settled next to a group of resentful Kurds who had been forced out to make room for them. The community they established there continues flourishing to this day.

Meanwhile, a second group of roughly two hundred Kirghiz who refused to participate in the Last Exodus broke away from Rahman Qul and returned to the Wakhan, where they resumed the migratory lifestyle of their forebears. Lost within the immensity of the High Pamirs the descendants of these Kirghiz now struggle to uphold an ancestral lifestyle that represents one of the last great nomadic horse cultures on earth.

As romantic as that may sound, life has been exceptionally difficult for the Wakhan Kirghiz, and their capacity to survive seems to grow more marginal with each passing year. Unable to migrate to the warmer lowlands, they are exposed to the full fury of winters, which can last from September through June, with temperatures plummeting as low as negative twenty degrees. Despite the fact that the entire community often teeters on the threshold of starvation, especially during the early spring, they are cut off from even the most basic government services. As late as 1999, there was not a single school, hospital, dispensary, police station, bazaar, veterinary facility, post office, or doctor's clinic in the eastern sector of the Wakhan. Even by the extreme standards of Afghanistan, a country where 68 percent of the population has never known peace, the average life expectancy is forty-four years, and the maternal mortality rate is exceeded only by that of Liberia, the homeland of the Wakhan Kirghiz can be a desperate place.

The sole connection between the Kirghiz and the outside world is a single-lane dirt road that starts in the provincial city of Faiza-bad, in the Afghan province of Badakshan, and runs more than a hundred miles through the towns of Baharak, Ishkoshem, and Qala-e-Panj to the village of Sarhad, about halfway into the Corridor, where the road ends. Beyond Sarhad, all movement takes place on foot or on pack animals along narrow trails that hew closely to the Darya-i-Pamir and the Wakhan rivers and extend all the way to the easternmost end of the Corridor, where the frigid waters of a shallow, glassy blue lake lap at the edges of a grass-covered field known as Bozai Gumbaz. It was here, not far from the exact spot that Marco Polo spent the winter of 1272 recovering from malaria, that the Kirghiz leader who had dispatched his emissaries over the Irshad Pass to find me was hoping to build a school.

If any place met the definition of our last-place-first philosophy, surely this was it.

Needless to say, the logistics of even getting to such a location, much less constructing a place where teachers and students could gather to study and learn, were going to be daunting, especially for an organization as tiny as ours. Plus, there was enough work to keep us busy in Pakistan for the next fifty years. Prudence suggested that it might not be wise to spread our resources too thin by venturing into unknown territory at the far end of another country and attempting to work with communities we knew nothing about.

Then again, that's pretty much exactly what got us into this business in the first place. And besides, the team of people we've built up over the years tends to relish this kind of challenge.

As my wife often reminds me, I have a very unusual staff.

There are many unorthodox aspects to my style of operation, starting with my tendency to fly by the seat of my pants and extending through my willingness to fashion working alliances with unsavory characters who have included smugglers, corrupt government flunkies, and Taliban thugs. Even more unusual is my preference for employing inexperienced, often completely uneducated locals, whom I tend to hire solely on gut instinct—a practice, it turns out, that I learned from my father.

In the spring of 1958, when I was three months old, my parents moved our family from Minnesota to East Africa to teach in a girls' school and four years later helped establish Tanzania's first teaching hospital on the slopes of Mount Kilimanjaro. My sisters Sonja and Kari and I attended a school where the children hailed from more than two dozen different countries. Meanwhile, my father, Dempsey, struggled to lay the foundations for the Kilimanjaro Christian Medical Centre (KCMC).

His greatest challenge was to overcome the expat community's fear of empowering local people. He was told repeatedly that getting anything done in Africa required a *muzungo* (white man) wielding a *koboko* (a hippo-hide whip). Despite these prejudices, he never wavered in his conviction that the key to success was listening and building relationships. In lieu of tea drinking, he would head over to the nearby town of Mamba, where after Sunday church, male and female elders would sit in circles, passing around a communal gourd of *pombe* (banana beer) while they celebrated their friendship and resolved their problems.

Over a decade, my father slowly put together a team that resembled a miniature United Nations. The construction firm that built the hospital were Zionists from Haifa. The engineering consultants were Egyptian Sunnis. The architect was a Roman Jew, many of the senior masons were Arab Muslims from the Indian Ocean coast, the accountants were Hindus, and the project's inner circle of advisers and managers were all native Africans. Communication was a challenge during the early years, and there were several times when the whole thing almost fell apart. Nevertheless, my dad persisted, and by 1971 the KCMC was finally up and running—at which point he did something really interesting.

To celebrate the opening of the hospital, he built a giant cement barbecue in our backyard and held a daylong party, in the middle of which he stood up and gave a speech. After apologizing for all the hard work he had put everyone though, he thanked every single person who had been involved, from the top administrators down to the lowliest laborers, and praised them for a job well done. Then he said that he had a prediction to make. "In ten years," he declared, "the head of every department in the hospital will be a native from Tanzania."

There was an awkward moment of silence, and from the audience of expat aristocrats came a collective gasp of disbelief. *Who do you think you are?* they demanded. *How dare you boost these people's hopes with such unrealistic expectations and set them up for failure?* The explicit assumption was that it was naive and inappropriate to hold the Tanzanians to the same standards that westerners might expect of themselves. The implicit—and more insidious—assumption was that these Africans lacked ambition, competence, and a sense of responsibility.

Our family returned home to Minnesota in 1972, and in 1981 my father died of cancer. A year later, when the hospital's annual report for 1981 arrived in the mail, my mom showed it to me with tears in her eyes. Every single department head was from Tanzania, just as he had predicted—a fact that remains true today, twenty-eight years later.

One of my great regrets is that my father didn't live long enough to see that his instincts not only were vindicated, but also inspired some copycats. Because in my own way, I've adopted the very same approach in Pakistan and Afghanistan.

Altogether, the Central Asia Institute field staff totals about a dozen men, almost all of whom have appointed themselves to their positions. Even though I'm not the sort of person who normally travels with a security team, a hulking tribesman from the Charpurson Valley who once worked as a high-altitude porter on K2 (until his shoulder was torn to pieces in a car accident) insists on serving as my bodyguard. His name is Faisal Baig, and he embraces his duties with unapologetic fanaticism. In Skardu in the summer of 1997, Faisal caught a man leering through the window of the CAI Land Cruiser at my wife, Tara, as she was nursing our daughter, dragged him into an alley, and beat the poor man senseless.

Until a few years ago when he retired, the driver of that Land Cruiser was Mohammed Hussein. A gaunt-faced chain-smoker who could be moody and mercurial, Hussein took chauffeuring so seriously that he insisted on stashing a box of dynamite under the passenger seat—where I usually sit—so he could blast through the landslides and avalanches that often block the roads through the Karakoram. Our work was too important, Hussein believed, to waste time waiting around for government road crews.

Then there is Apo Abdul Razak, a tiny, bow-legged seventy-five-year-old cook who spent more than four decades boiling rice and chopping vegetables for some of the most famous mountaineering expeditions ever to climb in the Karakoram. Apo, who has fathered eighteen children and never learned to read or write, is so fond of tobacco that he smokes Tander cigarettes and uses chewing tobacco at the same time. (His few remaining teeth are the color of turpentine.) Apo's gift is his decency, which is infused with a sincerity so bottomless and so transparent that it endears him to everyone from Pervez Musharraf, the former president of Pakistan (who has taken tea with Apo on three different occasions), to the glowering security guards who are endlessly confronting us at airports, hotels, and highway checkpoints—and who often receive a hug from Apo after they are through patting him down for weapons. Also known as Chacha (uncle), Apo serves as the Central Asia Institute's senior statesman and diplomatic emissary, smoothing over disputes with recalcitrant mullahs, greedy bureaucrats, and bad-tempered gunmen.

It's true, I suppose, that our payroll includes one or two people whose qualifications might meet the definition of "vaguely normal." Haji Ghulam Parvi, for example, is a devout Muslim from Skardu who quit his job as an accountant with Radio Pakistan to become our chief operations manager in Baltistan. Mohammed Nazir, twenty-nine, an earnest young man with hooded eyes and a wispy goatee who manages several of our projects in Baltistan, is the son of a respected Skardu businessman who supplies food to the Pakistani troops bivouacked on the twenty-three-thousand-foot ridgelines looming above the Siachen Glacier, the highest theater of combat in the history of warfare. Most of our employees, however, are men whose résumés would never receive a second glance at a conventional NGO. The remainder of our payroll features a mountaineering porter, an illiterate farmer who is the son of a Balti poet, a fellow who used to smuggle silk and plastic Chinese toys along the Karakoram Highway, a man who spent twenty-three years in a refugee camp, an ex-goatherd, and two former members of the Taliban.

A third of these men cannot read or write. Two of them have more than one wife. And crucially, they are evenly divided between Islam's three rival sects: Sunni, Shia, and Ismaili (a liberal offshoot of the Shia whose spiritual imam, the Aga Khan, lives in Paris). I have often been told that under normal circumstances in Pakistan, it would be unusual to find men of such diverse ethnic backgrounds in the same room sharing a cup of tea. That may well be true. Yet with little pay and almost no supervision, they have somehow found a way to work together—and like the people at the end of the road whom they serve, they have accomplished some amazing things.

From the moment I set foot in Pakistan, I travel in the company of at least one or two of these men at all times. We spend weeks along the tortuous roads of Baltistan, Kashmir, and the Hindu Kush. Despite the long hours and the hard travel, they tend to exhibit the sort of behavior that makes me suspect they may actually belong to a roving Islamic fraternity. They often roar with laughter as they tease one another without mercy. Much of the humor is supplied by Suleman Minhas, a sharp-tongued, slickly mustached Sunni taxi driver who picked me up at the Islamabad airport one afternoon in 1997 and upon learning what I was up to, promptly quit his job and declared that he was now our chief fixer. Among the rest of the staff, Suleman is renowned for his symphonic snores, the gaseous emissions produced by his "other engine," and the mysterious splashing sounds that emerge whenever he's in the bathroom—a source of endless speculation and amusement among his colleagues.

Another popular source of diversion involves booting up our solar-powered laptop with SatLink capability and watching YouTube videos of firefights between the U.S. military and the Taliban. The hands-down favorite features a militant crying *Allah Akbhar*! (God is great!) while loading a mortar shell in backward and accidentally blowing himself to pieces. Apo, a pious Sunni who detests religious extremism, is capable of watching this video ten or fifteen times in a row, cackling with glee each time the explosion takes place.

The other big pastime revolves around teasing Shaukat Ali Chaudry, an earnest schoolteacher with a shy smile, gold-rimmed glasses, and an enormous black beard who fought with the Taliban before becoming one of our part-time freelance advisers in Kashmir. Having recently turned thirty in a country where most men are married by their late teens or early twenties, Shaukat Ali is behind schedule on the important business of finding himself a wife and starting a family. By way of addressing the problem, he recently sent out marriage proposals to no fewer than four different women—and, sadly, was turned down by all of them. Among the staff, these rejections are explained by Shaukat Ali's fondness for launching into long-winded and rather tedious religious monologues that often last up to forty-five minutes. The fastest way to resolve the marriage situation, his colleagues solemnly advise Shaukat Ali, would be for him to start courting deaf women.

If there were a Muslim version of *Entourage,* it would probably be modeled on my staff.

I often refer to this group as the Dirty Dozen because so many of them are renegades and misfits—men of unrecognized

47

talents who struggled for years to find their place and whose former employers greeted much of their energy and enthusiasm with indifference or condescension. But inside the loose and seemingly disorganized structure of the CAI, they have found a way to harness their untapped resourcefulness and make a difference in their communities. As a result, these men are performing a job that it would take half a dozen organizations to match, all of it fueled by their ferocious passion for women's education. To the members of the Dirty Dozen, schools are everything. Despite all the joking, they would lay down their lives to educate girls.

Even for a crew like this, however, the idea of setting up shop inside Afghanistan's Wakhan Corridor seemed, to put it mildly, somewhat insane. Pulling off such a feat would require a point man who possessed an unusual combination of physical courage and stamina, a mastery of at least five languages, and a willingness to travel on horseback for weeks at a time without taking a bath. A man who wouldn't mind crossing the passes of the Hindu Kush, unarmed and without fear, while carrying up to forty thousand dollars in cash in his saddlebags. Someone who could negotiate with warlords, heroin dealers, gunrunners, corrupt government officials, and some very shady tribal leaders—and when necessary, charm the hell out of these people.

Fortunately, we were just about to hire someone who fit the bill—a man whom I refer to as our Indiana Jones.

CHAPTER 2

The Man with the Broken Hand

Mountains can never reach each other,
despite their bigness. But humans can.
—AFGHAN PROVERB

Widow in Kabul, Afghanistan

PHOTO: © 2003 TERU KUWAYAMA

We met in the autumn of 1999 in the village of Zuudkhan, at the far end of the Charpurson, on the night before the Kirghiz horsemen came riding over the Irshad Pass. I had come to Zuudkhan ostensibly to inspect a project we had funded that involved laying a seven-kilometer-long pipe to provide the village with clean water and hydroelectricity. Normally, we don't involve ourselves in things like this, but it was the only way the government's inspector general would allow me into the Charpurson, which had been closed to foreigners since 1979 when the Soviets invaded Afghanistan. The real purpose of my visit, however, was to learn something about the Kirghiz, Wakhi, and Tajik communities just across the border in Afghanistan.

For the past two years I had been receiving sporadic reports that the people on the northern end of the Hindu Kush were desperate to begin educating their daughters. These messages suggested that several tribal leaders in the Wakhan Corridor had been attempting, without success, to get word to me—and Zuudkhan seemed like the most promising place to set up a communications link. In these same reports, I also kept hearing about a man in the Charpurson who might be able to help.

His name was Sarfraz Khan, and the stories that clung to him were both colorful and provocative. Some described him as a mishmash of contradictions: an ex-commando who was skilled in the arts of alpine combat, drove a "Taliban Toyota," loved music and dancing, and wore a peacock blue, Dick Tracy–style fedora in the mountains. Others hinted at a man with an unusual past: a smuggler of gemstones, an imbiber of whiskey, a trader of yaks. Outlandish claims were made about his marksmanship, his horsemanship, and his dentistry: It was said that he could take down an ibex with a high-powered rifle from a distance of up to a mile; that he could ride like a Cossack; and that when he took part in *bushkashi,* the violent central Asian version of polo played with the headless carcass of a goat, he did so with such passion and ferocity that his front teeth had been smashed to pieces, then replaced with dentures made of stainless steel.

There were some dark rumors of scandal, too: tales that spoke of a divorce from a first wife and, following on the heels of that disgrace, an even greater one arising from the unthinkable demand that he be permitted to gaze upon the face of his second betrothed before he would consent to marry her. Such a request was an appalling breach of propriety, yet if the stories were true, the request had actually been granted, the first and only time a demand so outrageous had ever been acceded to in the one-hundred-year history of Zuudkhan. What's more, no one could fully explain the reasons why—except, perhaps, as evidence of this Sarfraz Khan's prodigious charisma and his uncanny ability to command other men by bending their will to his own.

Who could say where the truth ended and the legends began? All I knew was that this was someone I needed to meet.

Snow was falling in earnest when I headed northwest from the town of Sost on the only road through the Charpurson. By the time I arrived in Zuudkhan, just before 9:00 P.M., the flat-roofed, mud-walled homes of the village were draped in white and the place looked like a scene out of *Doctor Zhivago*. I was traveling with Faisal Baig, the CAI's security man, who had been born and raised in Zuudkhan, and we were slated to spend the night with the family of Faisal's nephew, Saidullah, who was running several of our schools in the nearby Hunza Valley.

After ducking through the low doorway into Saidullah's home, we greeted his parents and settled cross-legged on some thick yak-wool rugs, leaning back against walls, which were coated in a layer of blackened soot that had the consistency of hardened molasses. Saidullah's sister, Narzeek, had just served a thermos of hot tea when the door swung open and in blew a man clad in a cavernous Russian tundra jacket who looked as if he had just clawed his way out of bed and run a salad fork through his hair. As he came swishing into the room, he seemed preoccupied with the dial on a plastic radio that was blasting a Uighur rock-and-roll station from Kashgar, in western China. Then he spotted me through the blue haze of the yak-dung fire and promptly forgot about the radio.

"Ah, Doctor Greg, you have arrived," he cried, flinging open his arms and flashing a wide grin that revealed a row of metallic teeth. "That is *baf* (excellent)!" He proceeded to wade across the sea of yak-wool rugs and envelop me in a massive bear hug before stepping back to shake hands.

It was then that I noticed the claw. Three of the fingers on his right hand had bent back on themselves in a manner that resembled the talons on a bird, and when we shook, he squeezed my hand with only his forefinger and thumb. I was curious about what could explain such an injury, but he had already performed an about-face, whipped back out the door, and disappeared into the night.

A moment later, however, he was back.

In his arms he carried an expensive red blanket from Iran that was apparently reserved for honored guests, and he insisted that I wrap myself in it. After I had settled the blanket around me, we shared our first cup of tea and I began to learn his story.

For the better part of the past forty-two years, Sarfraz had been, by his own testimony, "no much success." His first marriage had failed—a considerable embarrassment in Muslim culture— and his second marriage was approved only after he had lied to his prospective in-laws about not having children from his first marriage (in fact, he had two daughters) and then shocked them with the demand to see the face of their daughter prior to the wedding. He had also drifted through a series of marginal business dealings in locations stretching from the Karakoram to the Arabian Sea without managing to establish either a home or a solid future for himself. Most important, perhaps, he had failed to find a calling that drew out his innate abilities as a leader and an agent of change.

Born and raised in Zuudkhan, he would never get more than an eighth-grade education—acquired in a village at the opposite end of the Charpurson Valley that took five days to reach on horseback. The boarding expense at this school was a considerable burden for his father, Haji Muhamad, who drew a modest income as a border patrolman collecting customs levies. Nevertheless, Haji Muhamad and Sarfraz's mother, Bibi Gulnaz, were committed to their eldest son's education because an eighth-grade graduation certificate would qualify him to work as a primary-school teacher.

In accordance with this plan, Sarfraz finished his studies and duly went to work teaching first grade in Zuudkhan's very first elementary school. In good weather the students met outside, and in bad weather they gathered in the kitchen of the communal *jumat khana* (the Ismailis' place of worship). Within a year, Sarfraz had realized that he detested teaching and decided to enlist in the army, where he served as a commando in the Punjab Regiments' elite mountain force. Posted to Kashmir in 1974, he was wounded twice during a firefight with Indian troops. The first bullet grazed the side of his upper right arm, while the second passed directly through the palm of his right hand. The military doctors failed to repair the hand properly, and as paralysis set in, three of his fingers folded permanently around themselves to form the distinctive crook that is now his trademark. (Despite the impediment, he retains the ability to hold a pen, shoot a rifle, and manipulate the steering wheel of a speeding Land Cruiser while gabbing on his cell phone.)

Sent home with an honorable discharge and a four-dollar monthly pension, Sarfraz resumed teaching in Zuudkhan but lasted only a year because of his poor pay and expanding family. He then moved to the nearby town of Gilgit, where he became a minivan driver on the treacherous Karakoram Highway, often driving for thirty hours straight and rarely going home. Plagued by *no much success,* he moved on to Karachi, Pakistan's largest city and its commercial center, where he landed a job as a *chokidar* (security guard) for six months. Then it was north to Lahore, the country's academic and cultural center, to work in a Chinese restaurant. *No much success* there either, and by the early eighties Sarfraz was on the move again, this time to Peshawar, the capital of Pakistan's volatile Northwest Frontier Province, where he worked as a chauffeur, mechanic, and auto broker before deciding, once and for all, to give up on cars. Out of options, he returned home to Zuudkhan—completing a circle that is familiar to millions of men who come from Pakistan's tribal areas, where the unemployment rate hovers around 80 percent.

By this time, the Soviet Union's occupation of Afghanistan

was in full swing. When the Soviets dispatched a squadron of helicopters across the border and into the skies above Zuudkhan, Pakistan's government responded by declaring the Charpurson Valley a security zone and closing it to all outsiders. Sensing an opportunity, Sarfraz decided to take up trading over the border with Afghanistan by leveraging his family's connections inside the Wakhan Corridor. (A century earlier, Sarfraz's ancestors had moved to the Charpurson Valley from the Wakhan, and many members of his extended family remained in the Corridor.)

He spent the next decade as a high-altitude trader. Three or four times a year, he would work his way over the Irshad Pass on horseback or on foot, ferrying rice, flour, sugar, tea, cigarettes, cooking oil, knives, batteries, salt, pots and pans, chewing tobacco, and anything else the inhabitants of the Corridor might need to make it through the winter. These items would be exchanged for butter and animals—mainly yaks and fat-tailed sheep—which he would drive back over the pass. He was also not averse to smuggling the occasional consignment of gemstones or whiskey, though he steered clear of opium and guns.

It was a hard way to make a living, even when it was supplemented with sporadic employment as a high-altitude mountaineering porter on K2 and other nearby peaks. Nevertheless, these experiences imbued Sarfraz with an impressive skill set. He came to know not only the nuances of the terrain and the movements of the Afghan and Tajik military patrols (which he avoided) but also the habits of the wild animals, especially the ibex and the Marco Polo sheep (which he took great pleasure in hunting). In the process, he gradually built up a dense network of business associates within the villages and settlements north of the Hindu Kush. By the end of a decade, his linguistic repertoire had burgeoned to the point where he could speak seven languages: Urdu, Punjabi, Dari, Burushkashi, Pashto, English, and Wakhi.

Those gypsy years that Sarfraz had spent as an itinerant

jack-of-all-trades and as an alpine peddler may have been rich in adventure, but when he recounted them before me that night in Zuudkhan, he did not romanticize this *no much success* period of his life. In his view, his aimless wanderings and his lack of financial success seemed to underscore how difficult it can be for almost any man (or woman) with a streak of independence to find his place within the poor villages and the teeming cities of Pakistan.

For my part, however, I perceived something quite different— and far more valuable.

By now the hour had grown late and the other members of Saidullah Baig's household had begun dropping off to sleep. When I realized just how much Sarfraz knew about the far side of the Hindu Kush, however, I tossed another clump of dried yak dung onto the fire and told him that I wanted him to give me a crash-course tutorial on the Wakhan. How many people were living there, what tribe did they belong to, and what were their religious and political affiliations?

Sarfraz chuckled and replied that it wasn't that simple. It was true, he acknowledged, that there were only about five thousand residents in the Wakhan. But inside the Corridor's 120-mile stretch—which in places is less than twelve miles wide—one encountered three different communities, each with its own distinctive customs, traditions, and ethnic identity, speaking three different languages and adhering to two separate branches of Islam.

At the far eastern end were the Kirghiz nomads, who move with their herds along the alpine pastures above twelve thousand feet. Descendants of the horsemen who founded the Ottoman Empire, the Kirghiz are Sunnis who speak a cognate of Turkish— attributes that differentiate them from their Wakhi neighbors directly to the west. The Wakhi people, Sarfraz explained, are ethnic Tajiks who trace their ancestry back to the Persian Empire in modern Iran. They are sedentary farmers who grow barley, buckwheat, and potatoes along the river valleys at altitudes considerably lower than those where the Kirghiz dwell. The Wakhi speak a cognate of Persian, and they belong to the Ismaili sect of Islam. Finally, at the far western end of the Wakhan, where the Corridor spills into Badakshan, the northernmost province of Afghanistan, one finds a third community. Like the Wakhi, they are ethnic Tajiks. But instead of Ismaili, they are conservative Sunnis, and their languages, Tajik and Dari, are separate cognates of Persian.

When Sarfraz saw that I was struggling to make sense of these overlapping religious and linguistic characteristics, he seized a notebook, tore off a sheet of paper, and declared that he was going to draw a special map that would cut through the confusion. Like everywhere else in Afghanistan, he intoned, geography is far less important than relationships. If you want to understand the way things work in the Wakhan, the locations of the villages and the rivers and the roads really don't matter all that much. What *does* matter is who swears allegiance to whom. This is the key to grasping the way that power flows, he declared, and when you comprehend the dynamics of power, everything else falls into place.

Then he drew three circles across the page—left, right, and center—and in the middle of each circle he wrote a name. The Kirghiz were represented by the circle to the right (the east), and the name he wrote inside it was that of Abdul Rashid Khan. This was the headman who had refused to participate in the Last Exodus to Turkey in 1982 and elected instead to remain in the High Pamir with a small group of followers. The name inside the center circle (which represented the Wakhi people) was Shah Ismail Khan. His headquarters, Sarfraz explained, were in the village of Qala-e-Panj, halfway through the Corridor, and he took *his* orders from the Aga Khan, the supreme leader of the Ismailis. The left circle (the Tajiks) bore the name of Sadhar Khan, a mujahadeen commander who had spent ten years fighting the Russians and another five years fighting the Taliban.

Power flows from west to east, Sarfraz explained. The Tajiks have more money and better weapons than the Wakhi; the Wakhi are more productive farmers than the Kirghiz; and the Kirghiz have huge herds of sheep and yaks whose wool and meat are coveted by everyone else. Even though Sadhar Khan is the strongest leader in the entire Corridor, the civil affairs of the Wakhan hinge on a delicate balance between him, Shah Ismail Khan, and Abdul Rashid Khan, each of whom acts as a kind of supreme commander within his respective sphere of influence. Nothing takes place inside the Corridor that does not escape the knowledge of these three "big men." No new venture unfolds without their permission.

When Sarfraz had finished laying all of this out, he plunged into a topic that held far greater interest for him than the human dynamics of the Wakhan. "And now we will discuss horses," he announced, growing visibly animated. "Because for the people of the Wakhan, nothing is more important!"

As the night wore on, we talked of serious equine matters: the beauty of horses, their capacity to elevate the status of those who can master them, the importance of the violent games that the men of this region play on horseback in order to demonstrate their courage and prowess. By the time we had exhausted this topic, it was nearly dawn. Before breaking off for the night, however, Sarfraz said he had a suggestion to make.

"If you are truly interested in the Wakhan," he said, "then tomorrow let me take you to the entrance to Irshad Pass, and you will be able to see the route that leads into the Corridor." And with that, he bid me good night and slipped out the door to return to his home.

That was the first of what would eventually become an endless string of conversations between Sarfraz and me. At the time, I now believe, he regarded me as nothing more (and nothing less) than an eccentric American with a lust for adventure who offered the chance for him to earn some cash. What I saw in Sarfraz, however, was a man who possessed energy, ambition, and a rather flamboyant sense of his own theatricality—and who seemed to be genuinely intrigued by our last-place-first approach to building schools, perhaps because it mirrored something in his own soul.

I also knew that I was in the presence of a proud, innovative, frustrated, and immensely competent man who seemed to be conducting his life as if it were an endless *bushkashi* match. In short, I recognized a spirit that was not kindred to my own so much as its complement. In ways that neither Sarfraz nor I fully understood at the time, each of us seemed to round out and finish off something inside the other.

And so it was that our conversation on that snowy evening in Zuudkhan marked the beginning of the greatest friendship of my life.

The following day, after the elders of the village had taken me on a tour of their new water pipe and the hydroelectric generator whose construction the Central Asia Institute had financed, Sarfraz and I clambered into his cherry red Land Cruiser and drove north on a horrendous road whose surface was coated with a gelatinous soup of ice, mud, and loose boulders. Our destination was Baba Gundi Ziarat, a small hexagonal shrine at the edge of Pakistan's northern border, on the threshold of the Afghan frontier.

It took an hour to complete the fifteen-mile trip, which took us through a barren landscape of treeless, rock-strewn hills that resembled the surface of the moon. The bleakness of the Char-purson (which translates to "place of nothing" in Wakhi) was hardened even further by the weather, a frigid mixture of sleet and snow that was periodically turned horizontal by the strong gusts of wind coming off the Hindu Kush.

As we drew near the shrine, we spied a herd of roughly twenty yaks, tended by five men on horseback. A group of Kirghiz had apparently just come through the Irshad Pass for a final trading session before winter set in.

These men were Sarfraz's friends and acquaintances, so after a round of introductions had been made, we gathered up several yak-wool blankets and spread them on the wet ground. It was while we were sitting there drinking salt tea that the squadron of fourteen Kirghiz riders, the men who had been sent out by Abdul Rashid Khan to find me, abruptly thundered around the corner at the entrance to the pass.

Their leader was Roshan Khan, the oldest son of Abdul Rashid Khan, and when we had finished exchanging pleasantries, Sarfraz leaped into the back of his Land Cruiser and presented the Kirghiz with forty bags of flour as an early celebration of Id (one of the two biggest holidays on the Islamic calendar). When the cargo was unloaded, we headed back toward Zuudkhan, sur-rounded by the horsemen.

We were back at the village by early evening and converged on Sarfraz's mud-walled home. While the Kirghiz dismounted and tended to their horses, Sarfraz selected a fat *mai* (sheep), dropped it gently to the ground with its head pointing southwest toward Mecca, said a quick blessing, and drew a knife across its throat. When the animal had finished bleeding out, Sarfraz's wife, Bibi Numa, removed the skin from the carcass and set about pre-paring the meat.

By nightfall, nearly forty people had crammed into Sarfraz's one-room, sixteen by twenty-foot home and arranged themselves with their backs to the walls. The Kirghiz sat cross-legged in their enormous boots, from which they pulled out their riding knives to serve as silverware. (It is generally forbidden to wear shoes inside someone's home, but Sarfraz had given the Kirghiz a special dispensation because if they removed their boots, their feet would swell up as a result of the high-altitude crossing they had just completed, and it would be almost impossible to get their boots on again.)

Most of the mutton had been boiled in a large pot, although a small portion had been fried into kebabs in a pan. The real delicacy, however, was the *dumba,* the blubberlike fat from the animal's tail and its hind end. This was placed on a platter in the center of the room, where it sat quivering like a hunk of golden Jell-O.

The Kirghiz inhaled this feast with the harrowing relish of men who had been subsisting on rainwater and chewing tobacco. They scooped up the fat with their fists, they stripped the meat from the bones with their riding knives, and they snapped the bones in half and sucked the marrow into their mouths with moist slurping sounds. Everything was consumed—the head, the testicles, the eyeballs—and when they were through, the men took their hands, which were now slathered in grease, and carefully smeared them over their faces, their hair, and their beards.

Later, when everyone had pronounced himself sated, Chinese thermoses filled with salt tea were brought in, followed by large bowls of *arak,* fermented mare's milk. Then it was time to prepare for bed, and as blankets were brought to Sarfraz's home from all over the village, the guests stepped outside to perform final ablutions.

By this time, the wind was settled, the snow had subsided, and the sky was littered with a spray of constellations so dense and so bright that the milky glow of the heavens defined every inch of the ridgelines along the peaks surrounding Zuudkhan.

As the horsemen squatted in the starlight cleaning their teeth with matchsticks or the tips of their knives, Roshan Khan stood beside me for a moment, looking up at the night sky. Then, with Sarfraz translating so that I could follow, he said that he had a message from his father that he needed to recite:

> *For me, a hard life is no problem. But for our children, this life is no good. We have little food, poor houses, and no school. We know you have been building schools in Pakistan, so will you come and build the same for us in Afghanistan? We will donate the land, the stones, the labor, everything that you ask. Come now and stay with us for the winter as our guest. We will take tea together. We will butcher our biggest sheep. We will discuss matters properly and we will plan a school.*

I replied that I was honored by this invitation, but I could not possibly return over the Irshad Pass to camp out with Abdul Rashid Khan for the next five months. First, I had no formal permission to enter Afghanistan—and the Taliban, who ran the government in Kabul, weren't exactly handing out visas to U.S. citizens. More important, my pregnant wife was expecting me home, and if I did not return soon, she would be deeply upset. Surely the Kirghiz could understand the seriousness and the magnitude of a wife's displeasure?

Roshan Khan nodded gravely.

However, I continued, I would definitely come to visit them when I got the chance, and when I arrived, I would do my best to help them. In the meantime, I needed some information. Could Abdul Rashid Khan perhaps give me a rough sense of the number of children, ages five to fifteen, who needed education?

"No problem," Roshan told me. "Soon we will give you the name of every single person inside the Wakhan."

This seemed a bit far-fetched. In the region that these men had just ridden out of, there are no phones, no faxes, no e-mail, no postal system, and no roads. Moreover, thanks to the snow and the storms, the area was about to be sealed off from the rest of the world for seven months.

"How in the world do they propose to get this information to us?" I asked, turning to Sarfraz. "And when it comes time for us to enter Afghanistan and make our way up to the Wakhan, how can we tell Abdul Rashid Khan when we're coming?"

"No problem, we do not need to tell," Sarfraz replied airily. "Abdul Rashid Khan will find a way of getting us the information. And he will know when we are coming."

Having no other alternative, I shrugged and took him at his word.

Now Roshan Khan and I enacted a ritual that I recognized from six years earlier, when Haji Ali had stood in the barley fields of Korphe and asked me to provide an assurance that I was coming back to him. The leader of the Kirghiz horsemen placed his right hand on my left shoulder, and I did the same with him.

"So, you will promise to come to Wakhan to build a school for our children?" he asked, looking me in the eye.

In a place like Zuudkhan, an affirmative response to a question like that can confer an obligation that is akin to a blood oath—and for someone like me, this can be a real problem. As those who work with me in the United States understand all too painfully, time management is not my strong suit: Over the years, I have missed so many plane flights, failed to appear at so many appointments, and broken so many obligations that I long ago stopped keeping track. But education is a sacred thing, and the pledge to build a school is a commitment that cannot be surrendered or broken, regardless of how long it may take, how many obstacles must be surmounted, or how much money it will cost. It is by such promises that the balance sheet of one's life is measured.

"Yes," I replied. "I promise to come and build you a school."

The next morning by five o'clock, they were gone. It would be five years before we saw each other again.

CHAPTER 3

The Year Zero

But it was the women who burned the eyes with tears.
The Taliban had hated them.
—COLIN THUBRON, *Shadow of the Silk Road*

Girls' school bombed by Taliban in Baujur, NWFP, Pakistan

*I*f the band of Kirghiz horsemen riding north toward the Irshad Pass on that October morning seemed to belong to the thirteenth century, the Afghanistan they were returning to was trapped in a modern-day Dark Age in which civil society was under siege and time itself seemed to be moving backward.

Ten years earlier, the country had shattered into a patchwork of isolated fiefdoms as the rival mujahadeen militias who had been responsible for driving the Soviet army back beyond the borders of the USSR started battling one another for power. During the early 1990s, virtually every town and district in Afghanistan descended into unbridled lawlessness. The main roads connecting the cities of Quetta, Herat, Kabul, Jalalabad, and Mazar-i-Sharif were choked with hundreds of extralegal checkpoints, each manned by a petty chieftan or a band of young fighters armed with a few Kalashnikovs who would demand payments from travelers. In towns such as Torkham and Kandahar, young boys and girls were regularly abducted and pressed into servitude or raped. Merchants and shopkeepers were forced to contend with gangs that indulged in looting, extortion, and murder. The arbitrary nature of these crimes and the chaos they unleashed eventually gave rise to an atmosphere of widespread public revulsion, fear, and betrayal.

Then in October 1994, a group of about two hundred young men, many of whom had grown up in the squalid refugee camps around the city of Peshawar, joined forces to launch a new jihad. The vast majority of these men had studied in hard-line madrassas, or religious schools, sponsored by Saudi Arabian donors or the government of Pakistan, where they had been indoctrinated with a virulent and radical brand of Islamist ideology. Calling themselves the *Taliban,* a Pashto word that means "student of Islam," they crossed the Pakistan border and swarmed into the Afghan truck-stop town of Spin Boldak with the aim of restoring righteousness and stability by uniting the country under the banner of a "true Islamic order."

The Taliban wore black turbans, flew a white flag, and swore allegiance to a reclusive, one-eyed Pashtun named Mullah Omar who made his headquarters in Kandahar and was rumored to anoint himself with a perfume he said was based on the recipe of the scent used by the Prophet Muhammad. During the next several weeks, their ranks rapidly swelled with new recruits until their numbers reached more than twenty thousand fighters. Aided by weapons, ammunition, and communications technology supplied by Pakistan's most powerful intelligence agency, they achieved a series of decisive victories against their mujahadeen rivals. Within a month they had stormed Kandahar and captured the town's airport, where they commandeered six MiG-21 fighter jets and four Mi-17 transport helicopters. By the following September, their motorized cavalry of Japanese pickup trucks mounted with machine guns had overrun the western city of Herat. A year after that, they took the eastern town of Jalalabad and then Kabul itself, where they seized Afghanistan's

Communist leader and former president, Mohammad Najibul-lah, castrated him in his bedroom, tied him to the back of a Land Cruiser, and dragged him round and round the compound of the palace before hanging his body from a traffic post for all the city to see.

By the end of 1996, the Taliban controlled over two-thirds of the country and had established a draconian regime that blended sadism with lunacy. Bizarre edicts where issued that forbade people from listening to music, playing cards, laughing in public, or flying a kite. Marbles and cigarettes were taboo. Toothpaste was banned, along with sorcery and American-style haircuts—especially those that mimicked the look sported by Leonardo DiCaprio in the movie *Titanic*.

These new rules were enforced by thuggish officials from the "Department of the Promotion of Virtue and the Prevention of Vice," who patrolled the streets in pickup trucks wielding AK-47s or whips made of radio antennae. In their zeal to impose a new moral order, they created an atmosphere so austere that the only acceptable form of public entertainment was attending executions in which criminals were stoned to death in soccer stadiums or hung from street lamps. All across the capital city, a place once beloved for the songs of its nightingales, thrushes, and doves, anyone who dared to keep birds was imprisoned and the birds were slain.

In addition to their many other targets, the Taliban fiercely opposed anything deemed *bid'ah,* the Arabic word for innovation that leads to deviation from the Koran. As part of their campaign to sever virtually all contact with the outside world, they banned movies and videos, destroyed television sets by running them over with tanks, strung spools of music cassettes from lampposts, and decreed that anyone caught carrying a book that was "un-Islamic" could be executed.

Eventually, this violent catechism spilled over into an assault on the social and cultural fabric of Afghanistan itself. At the National Museum, which contained perhaps the world's finest collection of central Asian art, virtually every statue and stone tablet was smashed to pieces with hammers and axes—an expression of the Taliban's conviction that artistic depictions of living creatures help to promote idolatry. For the same reasons, they blew up two mammoth Buddhist statues in the province of Bamiyan that had been carved into the side of a sandstone cliff during the third and fifth centuries. Inside Kabul's presidential palace, the head of every peacock on the silk wallpaper was painted over in white, and the stone lions guarding the building's entrance were decapitated.

By the late 1990s, this inferno had begun to warp and consume even the most sacred principles at the heart of the Taliban's vision—the spirit of Islam itself. Islam is not simply a religious faith based upon the words of the Prophet Muhammad and founded on the principle of absolute submission to the will of Allah. Islam is also the framework of a civilization created by the community of Muslim believers—a framework that includes not simply theology but also philosophy, science, the arts, and mysticism. Whenever Islamic civilization has achieved its fullest and most beautiful levels of expression, it has done so in part because its leaders permitted the societies over which they ruled to be enriched by tolerance, diversity, and an abiding respect for both the divine *and* the human. By deliberately seeking to destroy this tradition, the Taliban—like many other contemporary Islamic fundamentalist groups—abandoned the message of the Koran to build a society that is just and equitable and whose rulers are directly responsible for the welfare of all their citizens.

Of the many ways in which the Taliban perverted and brutalized the tenets of Islam, however, nothing quite matched the crimes that they visited upon their sisters, daughters, mothers, and wives.

During the early 1970s, the women of urban Afghanistan enjoyed a level of personal freedom and autonomy that was relatively liberal for a conservative Muslim society. According to the U.S.-Afghan Women's Council, a significant percentage of the women in Kabul worked for a living—tens of thousands of them serving in medicine, law, journalism, engineering, and other professions. In the country's rural areas, of course, the opportunities for female education and employment were far more limited; but in Kabul itself, unveiled females could be seen inside factories and offices, on television newscasts, and walking the streets wearing Eastern European–style dresses and high heels. Within the first week of taking Kabul, the Taliban stripped away these privileges and summarily rendered the female population silent and invisible.

In every major city and town across the country, women were now forbidden to go outside their homes unless accompanied by a close male relative and clad in an ink-blue burka. The few who dared venture out in public were not allowed to purchase goods from male shopkeepers, shake hands with or talk to men, or wear shoes whose heels made a clicking sound. Any woman who exposed her ankles was subject to whipping, and those who painted their nails could have the tips of their fingers cut off. Young girls were banned from washing clothing in rivers or other public places, participating in sports, or appearing on the balconies of their homes. Any street or town that bore the name of a female had to be changed.

As these injunctions against women piled up, unforeseen contradictions gave rise to even more grotesque levels of absurdity. Women who were ill, for example, could be treated only by female doctors—yet during the first week after the Taliban seized Kabul, all women physicians were confined to their homes and denied permission to go out, thereby severing half the population's access to health care. Those same restrictions also meant that the capital city's war widows who had no living male relative—a group whose numbers the USAID estimated to exceed fifty thousand—suddenly had no way of earning a living except through begging, stealing, or prostitution. Those enterprises, of course, were violations of the law that merited punishments ranging from beating and amputation to being stoned to death, depending on the whims of the religious police.

One of the primary targets in this war against women was, quite naturally, education. The moment the Taliban captured Kabul, every girls' school and university in the country was abruptly closed, and the act of teaching girls to read and write was outlawed. In the capital city alone, this resulted in the immediate suspension of 106,256 elementary-school girls and more than 8,000 female university students. In the same moment, 7,793 female teachers lost their jobs. To enforce this policy, the vice-and-virtue squads started carrying rubber whips made from bicycle tires that were specifically designed to be used on girls attempting to attend class. Any teacher caught running a clandestine girls' school was subject to execution, sometimes directly in front of her students.

In response to such outrages, a handful of women resisted by setting up an underground network to provide health care, education, and a means of communicating with the outside world. Groups that included the British government's Department for International Development, Save the Children, and the Swedish Committee for Afghanistan helped courageous women set up secret schools for girls in houses, offices, and even caves. By 1999, some thirty-five thousand girls around the country were being homeschooled. Despite these developments, however, the experience of finding themselves imprisoned in small apartments and cut off from all aspects of public life began to take an appalling toll. In a health survey of Afghan women conducted by Physicians for Human Rights in 1998, 42 percent of the respondents met the diagnostic criteria for post-traumatic stress disorder, 97 percent displayed symptoms of major depression, and 21 percent revealed that they experienced thoughts of killing themselves "quite often" or "extremely often."

Under the sorts of conditions imposed by this fanatical theocracy, the idea that an ex–mountain climber from Montana might consider venturing into Afghanistan in order to start building schools and promoting girls' education was, quite simply, unthinkable. By the summer of 2001, however, the Taliban's fortunes were poised to suffer a radical reversal.

Several years earlier, having already been evicted from his native Saudi Arabia, Osama bin Laden had been expelled from his base in Sudan along with his wives, his children, and scores of his closest followers. With the blessing of the Taliban leadership and the government of Pakistan, Bin Laden and his entourage had been permitted to settle in Afghanistan, where he had proceeded to plan and finance a series of terrorist operations, including the August 1998 bombings of the American embassies in Kenya and Tanzania, which the U.S. State Department reported killed more than 230 people and wounded more than 4,000.

Although the Taliban leaders were clearly uneasy about Bin Laden's terrorist activities, they had rebuffed repeated demands by U.S. government officials that he be expelled from the country or handed over for trial. The Taliban's reasoning was straightforward: Bin Laden was a fellow Muslim who had fought with them against the Russians, and to turn him over to the Americans—or anyone else—would have violated the Pashtun code of *nenawatay*, the right of refuge and protection that is afforded all guests. This is where matters stood during the second week of September, 2001.

At the time, I had returned to Zuudkhan, Sarfraz Khan's village in the western part of the Charpurson Valley, in order to check up on a women's vocational center that we had recently established. On the second night of my visit, I stayed up quite late meeting with a group of community elders and didn't make it to bed until after 3:00 A.M. Sarfraz, as he often does, remained awake, fiddling with his Russian shortwave radio in the hope of catching his favorite radio station out of the Chinese city of Kashgar, which broadcasts the reedy Uighur music he loves to listen to. Instead, he picked up a disturbing news broadcast about an event that had just taken place on the other side of the world. Shortly after 4:30 A.M., Faisal Baig shook me awake.

"I'm sorry," he said. "A village called New York has been bombed."

The American response to the attacks on the World Trade Center and the Pentagon was swift and devastating. Operation Enduring Freedom, launched on October 7, involved both a massive aerial bombardment and a ground offensive spearheaded by a loose coalition of mujahadeen militias from northern Afghanistan who received the support of several hundred Central Intelligence Agency operatives and U.S. Special Forces. By November 12, the Northern Alliance had seized nearly all of the territory controlled by the Taliban and retaken Kabul. A month later, Taliban fighters abandoned their last stronghold in Kandahar, the southern city from which they had launched their original campaign to conquer the country. As the leaders scattered and ordinary fighters melted back into the villages or fled across the border to seek refuge in Pakistan's Tribal Areas, the movement of bearded clerics and earnest madrassa pupils that had swept across all but a tiny sliver of northern Afghanistan seemed to vanish into thin air. And so it was, in the second week of December, that I was finally able to pay my first visit to Kabul.

The road from Pakistan to the Afghan capital is on the west-

ern end of the 1,600-mile Grand Trunk Highway, which is one
of South Asia's longest and oldest major roads, dating back to
the Mauryan Empire that began in 322 B.C. The Grand Trunk
was originally a series of trade routes that linked the Bay of Bengal and present-day Pakistan to Afghanistan and the Persian
Empire. Over centuries, dozens of successive empires used this
route to move armies ranging from foot-soldier infantries and
elephant-mounted cavalries to mechanized tank divisions.

My trip started out with Suleman Minhas driving me through
the western suburbs of Peshawar and past a check post featur-
ing a twenty-year-old signboard that declared NO FOREIGNERS
ALLOWED BEYOND THIS POINT. From there, the road heads up into
the Safed Koh Mountains, a perilous twenty-three-mile stretch
that needs to be navigated with precision to dodge oncoming traffic from both front and rear. (Some locals call this section of the
Grand Trunk the Martyr's Road because so many drivers have
been killed in accidents or by bandits.) This segment concludes
at the town of Landi Kotal, which features a smuggler's bazaar
where one can purchase everything from tires to television sets
to heroin. Directly off the road in Landi Kotal is a colonial cem-
etery where hundreds of British soldiers who were slaughtered
during the Second Afghan War (1879–90) and the Third Afghan
War (1898 and 1919) are buried—a graphic reminder of the fate
that has befallen every foreign army that has ever attempted to
invade and control Afghanistan.

From there, the Grand Trunk begins a dramatic descent
toward the Afghan border. Along this steep and narrow incline,
overladen supply trucks shift down to their lowest gears as they
thread through the rust red limestone walls that mark the legendary Khyber Pass, through which armies from Alexander the
Great and Genghis Khan to the Persians, the Moguls, and the
British have passed. From the Khyber Pass, it is only about three
miles to the Afghan border and the town of Torkham.

In December 2001, Torkham was a frenzied circus of thousands of Afghan refugees, some of whom were returning to Afghanistan while others were heading back to Pakistan. One elderly Afghan man with a wispy beard told me he was fleeing Afghanistan due to the U.S. bombing campaign, while a woman with a handful of kids declared that she was evacuating because her land had been seized by squatters and she had nowhere to go. The actual border was an open circular area crowned on both sides by massive metal gates. The Pakistani immigration clerks' office featured dozens of official-looking filing cabinets. On the Afghanistan side, the arrangements consisted of a desk, a chair, and a single courteous official who gave me one look and performed a staccato of stamping on the surface of my passport. "Most welcome to Afghanistan," he declared with a big smile. "Can I give you some tea?"

So far, so good, I thought. *The first Afghan I meet offers a cup of tea.*

I politely tried to decline, but he insisted, and after he barked an order out the back door, two small cups of steaming green tea were handed to us by a disheveled boy. After thanking him for his hospitality and bidding him farewell, I drove through the checkpoint and entered Afghanistan, where I found myself greeted by a mile-long line of metal shipping containers whose sides were pockmarked with bullet holes. From the interior of each container, entrepreneurs were hawking televisions, kites, music cassettes, and a host of other products that had been forbidden under the Taliban.

Driving past this Afghan-style shopping mall, I was offered a more sobering reminder of the wars that had been raging unchecked here for the past twenty-two years. As far as my eye could see, the sides of the Grand Trunk Highway and the surrounding hills were littered with the carcasses of tanks, artillery launchers, and armored personnel carriers. Amid the detritus, I could pick out a scattering of rusted helicopters. They resembled the broken skeletons of dead birds.

Twelve hours later, when I finally reached the capital, the devastation was everywhere. Kabul in the winter of 2002 was effectively at "year zero": its population traumatized, its infrastructure destroyed, its suffering and its horrors etched upon the gray and shattered surfaces of what had once been its architecture. Regardless of which direction one looked, it was impossible to pick out a single building whose facade had not been honeycombed with blackened holes punched by grenades and rockets. Two decades of virtually uninterrupted fighting had made even the most dignified structures appear drunken, wounded, or lost. The entire city seemed to affirm the notion that warfare is a disease.

Amid this destruction, government officials conducted their business under burlap or plastic sheets tethered to the remains of the various ministerial buildings. Passing the airport, I could spot pieces of bombed planes lying by the runway, and demining crews were clearing the edges of the taxiways with armored bulldozers. The national airline, Ariana, was in shambles: After the U.S. bombs had knocked six of its old planes out of business three months earlier, only a single aging Boeing 727 remained operational. In the months to come, I would learn that Ariana's pilots and stewardesses who flew to New Delhi or Dubai were forced to sleep on the plane at night because the crew could not afford hotel rooms. The flight engineers used a slide rule to calculate weight and balance, and each flight had to carry cash in order to pay for fuel.

Eventually I made my way to a crumbling building on Bagh-e-Bala Road called the Peace Guest House. Snow had fallen, and there was no heat, electricity, or running water. The sparse surroundings reminded me of being in a remote mountain village in Pakistan, except that I was in a bustling city of 1.5 million. That first night, I lay in bed listening to the sporadic bursts of automatic weapon fire resounding across the city. After each volley, there was a brief lull of silence that was filled by a shrill chorus of howling dogs.

Over the next few days, I moved about the capital city with the help of a taxi driver named Abdullah Rahman, a man whose eyelids had been scorched away by an exploding land mine and whose hands had been so badly burned that he was unable to close them around his steering wheel. One of Abdullah's several jobs involved safeguarding three locked cases of books at the Military Hospital library. Every morning, Abdullah, along with six other librarians, would sign in to the register to mark their presence, sit together at a long desk for about an hour, and then leave at the directive of their boss. Abdullah had been doing this six times a week for twelve years, and for his services he was paid $1.20 per month. He told me that on average, about one book a week was checked out.

During the next week and a half, I toured around the city with Adbullah in an effort to get a sense of how much damage had been done to the capital's education system. Despite the fact that classes were scheduled to reopen later in the spring, only a handful of the 159 schools were prepared to receive students, and even these were in horrendous condition. In some cases, the buildings were so unstable that classes would have to be held outside or moved to metal shipping containers. In other cases, the students would have to scale crude ladders built from logs after the stairways had been destroyed.

Toward the end of my stay, I paid a visit to Dr. Ashraf Ghani, who was Afghanistan's minister of finance and a personal adviser to Hamid Karzai, who would soon be appointed to serve as the country's interim president. Dr. Ghani had received his graduate degree in anthropology from Columbia University and later pursued a successful career with the World Bank, but after 9/11 he had given up everything to return to Afghanistan and help his country get back on its feet.

When we met in his office, the minister informed me that less than a quarter of the aid money that President George W. Bush had promised to his country had actually been delivered. Of those funds, Dr. Ghani explained, $680 million had been "redirected" to build runways and bulk up supply depots in Bahrain, Kuwait, and Qatar for the upcoming invasion of Iraq. Afghanistan was now receiving less than a third of the per-capita assistance that had been plowed into reconstruction efforts in Bosnia, East Timor, or Rwanda—and of that, less than half was going to long-term development projects such as education. Moreover, to administer this inadequate stream of cash, a massively expensive bureaucracy had sprung up.

As bad as this sounded, I learned later that the situation was even more bleak. A significant amount of the development money offered by the United States was, it turned out, simply recirculating into the hands of American contractors, some of whom were paying Afghan construction workers five or ten dollars a day to construct schools and clinics whose price tags could exceed a quarter million dollars per building. Equally disturbing, almost none of the tiny amount of money that was actually reaching Afghan citizens in Kabul was flowing beyond the capital and into the rural areas, where the devastation was even greater and the need for assistance even more desperate. Twenty miles beyond Kabul's suburbs, most of the country was largely on its own—a state of affairs that seemed to be lost on Dr. Ghani, overwhelmed as he was by the devastation at his feet.

"Look around you—Kabul is a mess," he exclaimed. "We don't have enough buildings to live in, not to mention electricity, food, communications, plumbing, or water. At least in the countryside the people have land on which to grow crops and rivers to drink from. They can sleep in a tent under the stars wherever they please, and they have animals to eat."

He reached for a black book filled with contact information.

"So you should begin your work right here in the city," he continued, opening the book and running his finger down a list of names. "I know many good contractors that can help you."

Clearly, there was a compelling case to be made that the CAI should devote its limited resources to working in Kabul. Serving the girls of Afghanistan's ravaged capital city would be enough to keep us busy for the next two decades. The problem, however, was that I already had given my word to the Kirghiz—and in order to honor that commitment, I was going to have to find a way to disengage from Kabul and begin making my way toward the Wakhan.

"I'm sorry," I told him, "but our mission is to serve remote areas and to set up schools where none already exist."

"Well, young man, have it as you wish," said Dr. Ghani, clearly disappointed. "But as you will find out, the last thing the people in the remote areas want is schools."

"Thank you for the information," I replied. "But I still need to head north."

CHAPTER 4

The Sound of Peace

*Traveling in Afghanistan was like wandering through
the shadows of shattered things.*
—CHRISTINA LAMB, *The Sewing Circles of Heart*

Greg with schoolgirls in Lalander village, Afghanistan

PHOTO: © 2007 TERU KUWAYAMA

When the Kirghiz horsemen and I had met for the first time in the fall of 1999, I had told them I needed a rough count of the number of school-age children in the eastern Wakhan. More than a year later, a group of traders crossed over the Irshad Pass, rode into Zuudkhan, and delivered up to Sarfraz a sheaf of several dozen pages of yellow, legal-sized notebook paper, bound between two pieces of cardboard and wrapped in a purple velvet cloth. The pages contained the first comprehensive census of every single household in the Afghan Pamir, painstakingly recorded by hand with a black fountain pen. According to this document, in a total population of 1,942 Kirghiz nomads, there were more than nine hundred children under the age of nineteen who were cut off from any access to education and whose families spent the year roaming over an area of approximately one thousand square miles. Farther west, along the banks of the Amu Darya, the river that delineates the Russian and Afghan frontiers, there were also more than six thousand Wakhi farmers scattered among twenty-eight villages who, having received word of our pledge to the Kirghiz, were now apparently clamoring for schools for their own children.

When Sarfraz showed me this census, I was dumbfounded not only by its thoroughness but also by what the numbers revealed about the true scope of the demand for education in the Wakhan.

By this point, it was clear to me that Sarfraz's many years of wheeling and dealing throughout the Corridor qualified him as the perfect point man to ramrod this initiative—so I decided to offer him a job as the Central Asia Institute's "Most-Remote-Area Project Director" with a salary of two thousand dollars a year. It would be his responsibility, I explained, to coordinate our most far-reaching ventures at every level, from drinking tea with the elders in each community to hiring the masons and carpenters who would do the work. He accepted with enthusiasm, exclaiming that he was finally about to embark on an enterprise that would involve *much success.*

"So if we want to put things in motion in the Wakhan," I then said to him, "how do we figure out where to actually put the schools that we need to build?"

Sarfraz—who as always was one step ahead of me—promptly whipped out another sheet of paper with a list of eight locations. Langhar, Bozai Gumbaz, and Gozkhon I had heard of; the other five were new to me. Then he unfolded a map of northern Afghanistan and started pointing with his index finger.

"We will build *here* and *here* and *here* and *here* and *here* and *here* and *here* and *here*," he declared. "And once these schools are finished, the children will come."

That sounded straightforward enough, but he went on to explain that we had two problems. First, if we wanted to set up operations inside the Wakhan, it was necessary to enlist the permission and support of the network of "big men" who ran the affairs of the Corridor, which meant that we needed to figure out a way to get from Kabul to the northernmost part of Afghanistan and start building relationships.

The second problem was that Sarfraz did not yet have a passport—which meant that for the first phase of this new venture, I was going to be flying solo.

The northern province of Badakshan has always stood somewhat aloof from the rest of Afghanistan—an isolated region, cut off from the south by the soaring escarpments of the Hindu Kush, whose deepest cultural and historical links extend north into Tajikistan and Uzbekistan. Between Kabul and Badakshan, the dry, rust-colored plains of southern Afghanistan give way to the Pamir Knot, the great tangle of peaks that marks the point where the Himalayas collide with the Karakoram. It is an implacable geographic barrier, and thanks to this great divide, Kabul can sometimes seems more distant—and more foreign—than the remote central Asian khanates of Bukhara, Bishkek, and Samarkhand.

Harshly beautiful and horrendously poor, Badakshan has historical ties to the kingdoms beyond its borders mainly because some of the most popular trade routes linking China, Kashmir, and central Asia passed through this area—and it was along these thoroughfares that one of the province's few treasures was shipped to the outside world. For more than six thousand years, the mines of Sar-e Sang, forty miles north of the Panjshir Valley, have provided the world's most important source of lapis lazuli, the gemstone that lent its intense blue fire to the death mask of Egypt's King Tutankhamen, the official seals of Assyrian and Babylonian governments, and the paintings of Renaissance Europe. (The stone was ground into a powder to make the pigment the Venetians called ultramarine.) In ancient times, Badakshan's seams of lapis were mined by lighting fires in the tunnels and then cracking the hot rock by packing it with ice. In recent years, the mujahadeen commanders who control the mines have preferred the use of military explosives.

Until recently, Badakshan's only other source of wealth was opium. The terrain and climate qualify this as perfect poppy country: suitable soil, steep and well-drained hillsides, long hours of sunshine, and the right amount of rainfall. The province sits directly in the middle of the "heroin highway" that transports raw opium north into Tajikistan, then Tashkent, Moscow, and points beyond.

As in other remote parts of Afghanistan, Badakshan's political and economic power has traditionally rested in the hands of local warlords, or *commandhans,* who fulfill many of the functions of a centralized government: guaranteeing security, providing small-business loans, maintaining roads, digging wells, sitting as judge and jury, supporting education, and, of course, levying taxes. It was the *commandhans* who led the mujahadeen struggle against the Soviets from the moment the first Russian tanks clattered across the borders of Uzbekistan and Tajikistan in the winter of 1979; and it was these men who kept the resistance alive when the Taliban swept over the rest of the country during the mid-1990s.

Since Hamid Karzai was first appointed interim president in 2002, this hierarchy has remained unchanged. Nothing takes place inside Badakshan's rocky gorges, lush valleys, and highland plateaus—no business venture, no marital alliance, no negotiation with outside authorities—without the express permission and the blessing of the *commandhans.*

For the previous five years, the reigning *commandhan* in eastern Badakshan had been a mujahadeen by the name of Sadhar Khan, a man who possessed the mind of a West Point military tactician and the soul of a poet. Born in a tiny hamlet not far from the mouth of the Wakhan Corridor, he had hoped to become a historian and scholar but was forced to abandon those plans when the Russians invaded in 1979 and virtually every able-bodied man and boy within a hundred miles of Baharak fled into the surrounding mountains to join the resistance.

During the early years of the war, Sadhar Khan's speed and cunning often got him picked to lead quick, dangerous raids deep into enemy territory. Thanks to these exploits, he rose swiftly through the mujahadeen ranks and eventually emerged as a lieutenant of Ahmed Shah Massoud, the famous "Lion of the Panjshir," who was perhaps the most gifted and formidable mujahadeen to fight against the Soviets. In addition to his leadership and planning skills, Khan also acquired a reputation for ruthlessness and ferocity. Inside the northeastern corner of Badakshan, his power was absolute.

Khan's base lay just outside of Baharak, a town of about twenty-eight thousand people where the roads arriving east from the regional capital of Faizabad and north from the Panjshir Valley converge. There is also a third road in Baharak that provides the only motorized means of accessing the Wakhan—and thanks to this, Sadhar Khan was effectively the gatekeeper for the entire Corridor. Without him, it would be impossible to drive a nail or lay a single brick for a school anywhere between the Pamirs and the Hindu Kush.

"Before you do anything, you must first go to Baharak and speak to Sadhar Khan," Sarfraz advised. "He is the *chabi*."

He twisted his wrist—the key.

Northeast of Afghanistan's capital city, nearly every mountain pass through the Hindu Kush is over ten thousand feet and thus is locked down by snow for six months of the year. In the 1960s, however, a three-mile-long tunnel was drilled by Soviet engineers below the Salang Pass to create an all-season route linking

Kabul with Badakshan. The tunnel is reached by a winding road on which Soviet military convoys were ambushed repeatedly by mujahadeen units that specialized in dismantling trucks, artillery cannons, even tanks, and hauling them, piece by piece, over the mountains and back to the Panjshir Valley. In the spring of 2003, I headed through the Salang in a rented Russian jeep driven by Abdullah Rahman, the taxi-driving librarian with the scorched hands and eyelids, in the hope of paying my first visit to Baharak.

In the years to come, I would look back on the obstacles I encountered during that first trip north and understand that together they represented a kind of metaphor for what our "Afghan adventure" would be like. When we were driving through the tunnel, the dust and the fumes became so dense that we were forced to stop the jeep and get out. Hoping to find an exit, I climbed through a viaduct leading to the outside, stumbled into a field where the rocks had been painted bright red, and realized I was surrounded by land mines. (After I carefully retraced my steps and descended back into the tunnel, Abdullah and I eventually blundered through and resumed our drive.) Later on that same journey, we found ourselves caught in a firefight between opium smugglers and were forced to take cover in a roadside ditch. When the shooting subsided, I told Abdullah that it was too dangerous for him to continue, jumped onto the back of a truck, and hid myself beneath a pile of putrid animal hides headed to a leather-tanning factory.

In the end, I made it to Baharak but was forced by my schedule to turn around without having met Sadhar Khan, return to Kabul, and fly home to the United States. A few months later, however, I was back in Afghanistan, repeated the same journey, and upon arriving in Baharak, immediately started casting around for the *commandhan*. Standing in the middle of the market, I spotted a white Russian jeep packed with gunmen rolling toward me and flagged it down on the assumption that anyone who could afford such a vehicle in Baharak would probably know Sadhar Khan.

The driver, a small, elfin man with refined features and a neatly trimmed beard, got out to address me.

"I am looking for Sadhar Kahn," I said in broken Dari.

"He is here," the man replied, in English.

"Where, exactly?"

"I am *Commandhan* Khan."

Having anticipated being forced to spend a week waiting for a meeting with a man who did his business from behind a wall of gatekeepers and armed guards, I was momentarily at a loss for words.

"Oh, I am sorry," I stammered, realizing that I had failed to introduce myself in proper Afghan fashion. "*As-Salaam Alaaikum*, I have come from America—"

"I apologize, but right now it is time for prayers," interjected Khan. "Please get in and I will take you to a safe place while I go to the mosque."

He drove us through the bazaar and to the northern end of the town's center and parked in the middle of the road next to the Najmuddin Khan Wosiq mosque. While a handful of plainclothes guards surrounded the jeep and whisked Khan into the mosque, I was led by a single uniformed guard to the second story of a nearby office building. When the guard ushered me into a dingy, windowless room, I requested to be permitted to go up to the roof. He was a bit puzzled but ushered me up the stairs and invited me to sit on a reed mat, where I had a dramatic view of the Hindu Kush range. Turning my gaze down into the street, I watched as several hundred men streamed out of the bazaar and into the mosque for their afternoon prayers.

About thirty minutes later, the procession of men emerged from the mosque, led by Sadhar Khan and the local *ulema* (religious leader). As he stepped into the street, Khan looked up, spotted me on the roof, and pointed. I watched, startled, as several hundred pairs of eyes followed the motion of his hand toward me. Then Khan gave a wave and cracked a smile.

When he had joined me on the roof, I introduced myself and began to tell him the story of the Kirghiz horsemen and our meeting at the southern end of the Irshad Pass. Before I was halfway through, his eyes lit up with astonishment and he wrapped me in a fierce bear hug.

"Yes! Yes! You are Doctor Greg!" he cried. Word of the promise to the horsemen had already filtered out of the Wakhan and reached Sadhar Khan. "This is incredible. And to think, I didn't even arrange a meal or a welcome from the village elders. Forgive me."

Later that evening, after eating dinner, Khan invited me to the roof of his own house so that we could discuss plans. He told me how eager the communities in his jurisdiction were to have schools, as well as many other services that his people so desperately lacked. He told me about all the girls who had nowhere to study, not only in the Wakhan but also in Baharak and across eastern Badakshan. He spoke of the destruction that had been wreaked over the course of two wars—the first against the Soviets and the second against the Taliban—and how much rebuilding needed to be done.

"Look here. Look at these hills," he said as he pointed toward the mountains looming over the town, whose lower slopes were strewn with countless rocks and boulders. "There has been far too much dying in these hills. Every rock, every boulder that you see before you is one of my mujahadeen, *shahids*, martyrs, who sacrificed their lives fighting the Russians and the Taliban. Now we must make their sacrifice worthwhile."

He turned to me with a look of fierce determination. "We must turn these stones into schools."

The implication was clear. Sadhar Khan was more than happy

to allow us to assist the Kirghiz, and he was eager to help this effort in any way he could. But before we could work our way out to the farthest reaches of the Wakhan, we needed to start by helping him to address the needs of his own community, right here in Baharak.

That was how our relationship began.

Over the next two years, I made several more trips to Baharak in order to cement our ties with Sadhar Khan and plan the school that would open the door for us to enter the Wakhan itself. Each of these visits took place inside his headquarters in the tiny village of Yardar, about three miles outside of Baharak. Here Khan maintained two compounds. The first was a modern, two-story, Soviet-style bunker with discreet defensive features that included false doors and hidden holes through which gunfire could be directed. This is where Khan entertained his guests. The other dwelling, a cluster of three mud-brick buildings five hundred yards east of the guesthouse, which featured dirt floors covered with dozens of tribal rugs, was his actual family home.

Inside the confines of the meager boundary wall that ran around the perimeter of this property, the numerous members of Sadhar Khan's extended family all lived together, the same kind of "village within a village" that can be found anywhere in rural Afghanistan or Pakistan. The buildings were surrounded by fields of wheat, barley, spinach, and okra, while the edges of the irrigation canals were lined with neat rows of walnut, pistachio, almond, cherry, mulberry, apple, and pear trees. In the summer and fall, Khan would delight in plucking some of the choicest fruits and nuts from the trees and pressing them on his guests.

"Forget about war—farming is much better than fighting," he once declared when he grew tired of my endless questions about his years during the Soviet occupation. On another occasion, he apologized for the fact that the pear he had selected for me was not as sweet as he thought it should be. "Most of my trees are too young," he explained. "I am trying to catch up for the twenty-five years we lost when we were too busy with fighting to be able to farm."

Whenever I rolled through the entrance gate to Khan's compound, glassy-eyed after yet another harrowing thirty-hour drive from Kabul, I found myself surrounded by a scene that offered an incongruous blend of the ancient and the modern. It was almost always late afternoon or early evening when I arrived, and as smoke from the evening cooking fires filtered through the rays of the setting sun, the call of the muezzin resounded across the fields, punctuated by the tinkling of the little bells tied to the necks of cows and goats as small boys herded the animals home for the night. Meanwhile, a group of up to a dozen young men dressed in combat boots and army fatigues might be kicking a soccer ball near the entrance gate while their older comrades stood beneath the satellite dishes mounted to the thatched roofs, cradling AK-47s in the crooks of their arms and muttering into their cell phones.

If it was still daylight, Sadhar Khan usually met me beneath the branches of a massive walnut tree, where he held court on a cement platform that his men had built directly over the irrigation canal. He was a busy man, and there was almost always a line of several dozen people squatting at the edge of the dirt driveway patiently waiting for an audience. These petitioners might include a group of farmers who had fallen into a boundary disagreement and were hoping the *commandhan* could resolve their dispute or the widows of fallen soldiers coming to collect cash. Yet whenever I arrived, he would get up to exchange embraces, then usher me onto an enormous red Persian carpet, where we settled ourselves, cross-legged, in a nest of maroon pillows. Then the *commandhan* would pour green tea into a set of tiny porcelain cups while his bodyguards passed around dishes filled with raisins, pistachios, walnuts, and candy as a prelude to whatever business we needed to discuss.

Later, as darkness descended over the valley, I would be invited to walk with the rest of his visitors and family members across the compound and into the guesthouse's long, narrow dining room. Only men were admitted, and after everyone was properly seated, Sadhar Khan would walk in and we would all stand up to formally shake his hand, then wait until he was seated before we resumed our places. (If another guest or male family member arrived, the same ritual would be repeated.) Once these courtesies had been properly observed, a group of three or four younger men, led by the host's oldest son, would unfurl a red plastic tablecloth across the length of the floor, and upon this surface the banquet would be laid out. The dishes served were simple and delicious: lamb, chicken, dal, spinach, okra, tomatoes, cucumbers, and rice.

When the meal was finished, the oldest guest would offer up the *dua,* a blessing of thanks. As the words were spoken, everyone would cup his hands together, palms raised, and when the blessing was complete each guest would sweep his hands over his face and intone, "*Alhamdulillah*" ("praise be to God" in Arabic). Finally, cups of green jasmine tea with a small sprig of mint would be served, and then we would talk deep into the night.

These discussions could sometimes last until the muezzin sounded the morning call to prayer at 4:30 A.M., and it was during these rituals that I began to learn about Sadhar Khan's past and to gain a sense of the experiences that had shaped him, especially the war against the Soviets.

In the first several years following the Soviet invasion of Afghanistan, Khan and his mujahadeen had deployed a host of desperate guerrilla tactics in the hope of countering the Soviets' over-whelming technological superiority. Along the narrow mountain roads to the east of Baharak, for example, his men would leap from ledges or boulders onto the tops of passing tanks and smear handfuls of mud over the drivers' viewing ports, then fling Molo-tov cocktails fashioned from Coke bottles into the hatches. They also adopted ruses that included broadcasting the tape record-ings of prayer chants on loudspeakers as a way of luring Russian infantry patrols into ambushes. During those early days of the struggle, they fought with whatever weapons they had—scythes, rocks, and sharpened sticks. Striking when they were able, they fled into the mountains, where they hid in caves, surviving on roots or dried cheese and, when necessary, eating grass.

For this resistance, they were made to pay dearly. Anytime a Russian soldier was killed, civilians were forced to flee as their homes were bombed by helicopters conducting reprisal raids. During the first five years of the war, it was not unusual for mujahadeen units like Sadhar Khan's to suffer 50 percent casual-ties in battle, but the reprisals against their homes and families could be even more devastating. While women and children spent weeks living in caves in the hills around Baharak, ani-mals were machine-gunned, crops were torched, and fields were seeded with land mines in an effort to force the population into submission through hunger and starvation. Today many of the trails leading down to the streams are adorned with small stone cairns marking the places where children who were sent to col-lect water were killed by Soviet snipers.

As one of the most important commanders, Sadhar Khan fea-tured prominently on the Soviets' target list. During the decade in which the Soviets occupied eastern Badakshan, the village of Yardar was shelled more than sixty times. Even though every building in Khan's compound had been completely destroyed by 1982, the Soviets' Mi-24 helicopter gunships continued bombing what he called "my dead land" and seeding it with land mines more than a dozen times.

It was those helicopters, which the Afghans called *Shaitan-Arba* ("Satan's chariots"), that wreaked the greatest destruction on the mujahadeen. The Mi-24s would conduct "hunter-killer" sorties, flying in formations of up to eight gunships, attacking mujahadeen positions with a range of weapons that included S-8 rockets mounted with fragmentation warheads and 30 mm high-explosive grenade launchers. No amount of bravery or guile on the part of the rebels could overcome such overwhelming firepower—until 1986, that is, when the American Central Intelligence Agency started supplying the Afghan insurgents with shoulder-mounted Stinger missiles equipped with heat-seeking guidance systems that were shockingly effective at taking out the slow-flying Mi-24s. During the next three years, the CIA flooded Afghanistan with over one thousand Stingers, resulting in hundreds of helicopters and Soviet transport aircraft being shot out of the sky.

In eastern Badakshan, the first mujahadeen to succeed in shooting down a helicopter with a Stinger was one of Sadhar Khan's most important subcommanders, a man named Haji Baba, who is now married to one of Khan's daughters. During our visits under the walnut tree, I was given the chance to hear Haji Baba himself recount the saga of his exploit, in exhaustive detail, on several different occasions. Each telling was slightly different, and the longest of them lasted more than an hour.

From Sadhar Khan I also learned about the sacrifices that the residents of Baharak and the surrounding countryside had made, after having fought the Russians from 1979 to 1989, in order to prevent the region from being overrun by the Taliban between 1994 and 2001. Out of these conversations I came to know a man who seemed to embody many of the contradictions and complexities of his torn and ravaged landscape, and also a man who was not ashamed to express his love of poetry, solitude, and flowers. Early one morning, he invited me to walk with him five or six hundred yards to the bank of the Warduj River, where two enormous boulders are suspended over the rushing water. Here, he explained, he often retreated to spend a few minutes alone before walking to the mosque to perform his evening prayers. As we sat there on the rock, I asked him if he would mind answering a question.

"Please," he said, "ask anything."

"You are a busy man with enormous responsibilities," I said, "so why is it that you spend so much time just sitting here watching the river run by?"

Khan smiled to himself and said that I wouldn't understand the answer to my question because I had never fought in a real war. "You may be a veteran, but you are not a warrior because you have never fought in battle," he gently explained. Then he began to describe, in graphic terms, some of the horrors he had witnessed: the concussive shock of a grenade as it tears apart the body of a man he had shared breakfast with only thirty minutes earlier; the nauseating odor emanating from the flesh of another comrade incinerated by a rocket; the sound that escaped the lips of a man who was dying from infections because his commander lacked even the most rudimentary medical supplies to treat his wounds.

Unlike other mujahadeen, such as Haji Baba, who often cackle with delight when they recount the glorious struggle waged by the mujahadeen, Sadhar Kahn was neither gloating nor boastful. Instead, he described what it felt like to have a friend whom one has known since grade school bleed to death in one's arms and then dump his body into a shallow grave. He talked of the impossibility of a normal life for women and children during war. He spoke of the mounting litany of loss as a life that should have been devoted to worthwhile pursuits, such as reading or music or the cultivation of pear trees, is given over to the business of death.

We talked—*he* talked—for almost two hours that afternoon, and in the end, he said this: "Sitting here watching the water rush past is the only way that I can justify having gone to war. The reason that I fought the Soviets and then the Taliban was for moments such as the one we're having right now. Unless you have been inside the fire of a battle, this is something that you will never understand."

About a year later, during another one of our encounters, Khan said that he had been thinking of our conversation next to the river that morning and was worried that he had failed to answer my question. Then he handed me a piece of paper. He explained that he had written a poem that might, perhaps, have succeeded in capturing the sentiments that he had been trying to express.

Here is the translation, from Dari:

You wonder why I sit,
here on this rock,
by the side of this river,
doing nothing?

There is so much work to be done for my people.
We have so little food,
we have so few jobs,
our fields are in shambles,
and still there are land mines everywhere.

So I am here to listen to
the quiet,
the water,
and the singing trees.

This is the sound of peace
in the presence of Allah.
After thirty years as a mujahadeen,
I have grown old from fighting.
I resent the sounds of destruction.

I am so weary of war.

CHAPTER 5

Style Is Everything

"Greg is very important to me. Without him, I'd be nothing more than a guy who trades yak butter."
—SARFRAZ KHAN

Wakhi family hearth in Sarhad, Afghanistan

During our many encounters, Sadhar Khan was invariably a model of gracious and refined hospitality—and yet, for me at least, his wry smile and his elaborate rituals of courtesy somehow never quite managed to soften the intensity of his stare. His eyes were a merry shade of green and his laugh had a high-pitched timbre, but when he saw or heard something that displeased him, his face could darken into the kind of expression that made one want to take a step back. In such moments, he seemed to bear a disquieting resemblance to one of the Russian land mines he so despised: a small container, lying just below the surface, that housed the potential for enormous violence.

Despite this sense of menace, Khan ultimately personified the kind of man that I would encounter over and over again during my time in Afghanistan: a former mujahadeen who had emerged from the savageries of the Soviet occupation and the atrocities of the war against the Taliban with a desire to spend his remaining years repairing the damage to his community. Like almost all *commandhans*, he was savvy and shameless in the way he went about this, installing supporters and family members in plum jobs, dipping his hand into the lapis lazuli mines sixty miles south of Yardar, and exacting a stiff tariff from the heroin traffickers whose mule trains moved a significant chunk of Badakshan's opium supply through his territory on the way to the Tajik border. Unlike his more corrupt colleagues, however, he was implacably determined to plow the bulk of these profits directly back into the welfare of his people. For the veterans who had served under his command, he had constructed a thriving bazaar in Baharak. He disbursed small loans so they could start businesses, helping to ease the transition from soldier to merchant, and handed out seeds and tools to almost any farmer who even hinted at needing help.

His special passion, however, was education, especially for girls. For almost twenty-five years there had been virtually no schooling in the rural villages of his region, and the loss this represented to the current and upcoming generations weighed on him deeply. "War has forced us to starve not only our bodies but also our minds," he once said to me. "This should never again happen to my people."

Unbeknownst to Sadhar Khan, the Central Asia Institute was about to be hit by a tsunami of cash that would enable us to take a dramatic step forward. In April 2003, *Parade* magazine ran a cover story about our school-building initiatives in Pakistan, and during the ten months following the publication of that story, our Bozeman office was flooded with more than nine hundred thousand dollars in donations. I had wired most of those funds to our bank in Islamabad and ordered the Dirty Dozen to embark on a score of new projects inside Pakistan, but I had also reserved a portion of the *Parade* money to launch our Wakhan initiative. In the spring of 2004, I informed Sadhar Khan that we were ready to begin building in Baharak.

As we sat on the red carpet under his walnut tree, I laid out exactly how the finances and other matters would be handled, explaining that these aspects of the project would not be subject to negotiation, even with a *commandhan* of his stature, because they were the only ways of guaranteeing that our projects are properly supervised and accounted for. The *shura* (local council of elders) in Baharak would be in charge of the funds, I told him, and he and his neighbors would be required to donate the land for the school. We would hire exclusively from within the local community for the basic labor, and we had budgeted fifty thousand dollars for construction and teachers' salaries, plus another ten thousand dollars for supplies, furniture, and uniforms. We would deliver one-third of this financing up front, in cash. Another twenty thousand dollars would be paid only after the workers had finished the construction to roof level, and the last payment would be delivered upon completion. As a final condition, at least 33 percent of the students would have to be female from the first day of class, and this number would need to increase each year until the girls' numbers reached parity with the boys'.

"Only 33 percent female enrollment?" Khan exclaimed, shaking his head and chuckling. "The number of girls waiting to attend this school is already almost double that, so perhaps you should consider giving our local council of elders a performance bonus for already exceeding your quota, no?"

I handed over the first down payment to the *shura* that morning, and work started immediately. By midafternoon the grid lines of the outer walls had been marked with twine and a crew of laborers was digging the trenches for the foundation with picks and shovels. Toward the evening, a series of explosions echoed between the walls of the surrounding mountains as the masons began dynamiting the granite boulders that would yield the stones for the walls. For Sadhar Khan, the reverberation of those blasts—which sounded eerily similar to Soviet or Taliban artillery—must have offered a deeply satisfying confirmation that we were truly turning stones into schools. For me, however, those concussive bursts signaled something else.

The door to the Wakhan Corridor was now unlocked, and it was time for Sarfraz and me to plan our next move.

When Sarfraz and I drew up our 2004 plan for northeastern Afghanistan, it was fairly straightforward. Since the only road into the Wakhan began in Baharak and ended halfway through the Corridor at the village of Sarhad, we decided on a two-pronged attack in which we would hit the beginning and end of the trail first, then literally build our way toward the middle until the literacy gap was closed. Once this process was complete, we would embark on the far more challenging task of leapfrogging into the roadless reaches at the far end of the Wakhan and fulfilling our commitment to the Kirghiz.

By this point, we had finally managed to get Sarfraz his first passport, and he had flung himself into a series of grueling trips from Kabul to Faizabad, through Baharak, and into the Wakhan in order to negotiate, launch, and supervise the first wave of school projects. Many of these journeys were solo undertakings, but whenever I flew into Kabul, Sarfraz and I would travel together—and it was during these ventures that our connection and our friendship began to deepen into something we both found rather remarkable. The chemistry we shared enabled us to understand each other so well that before long, each was able to anticipate the other's moves and complete his sentences. Eventually, we even got to the point where we communicated using a nonverbal vocabulary of glances and facial expressions. This did not happen immediately, however—and before we achieved this level of synthesis, it was first necessary for me to pass through a kind of cultural version of Afghan boot camp: a series of tutorials, run by Sarfraz, that I now refer to as Style School.

Starting with our very first trip north from the capital, I learned that traveling with Sarfraz through Afghanistan would be a far more complex and perilous affair than in Pakistan. Among the new concerns we faced, the biggest involved getting kidnapped. At the time, the going rate for bribing someone to help set up the abduction of an American citizen was around five million Afghans, or roughly $110,000. (Today, that number has increased tenfold.) To avoid this danger, Sarfraz was willing to go to extraordinary lengths, starting with camouflage.

Afghanistan is one of the most ethnically complicated countries on earth, a place where the overlapping cultures, languages, religions, and tribal loyalties have bedeviled historians, anthropologists, and military strategists for centuries. Understanding these distinctions was an essential precondition to safe travel, and this accounted for Sarfraz's obsession with a word that normally applies to the sartorial and behavioral nuances displayed on the streets of Manhattan or Paris, as opposed to the deserts and mountains north of the Hindu Kush. "To have much success in Afghanistan, you must understand style," he would patiently lecture me again and again. "Style is everything here."

In any given situation, regardless of whether it involved an all-night negotiation with a group of conservative mullahs or a five-minute break at a roadside tea stall, he paid keen attention to the body language of everyone involved. Who sat where and why? Who sipped his tea first and who hung back? Who spoke and who remained silent? Who was the most powerful person in the room, who was the weakest, and how did their respective agendas influence what they were saying? There can be many layers and shades of meaning within each of these distinctions, and by responding to them all with equally subtle adjustments of his own, Sarfraz strove to avoid drawing unwanted attention either to himself or to me. As a means of blending in as we moved from one region to another, for example, he often adopted different headgear, donning a *lunghi* (a Pashtun wrap-around turban) in the Taliban areas of Wardak province, exchanging it for a mujahadeen's *pakol* (woolen hat) in the Tajik-dominated areas of Badakshan, and eventually discarding that for a *kufi* (a white skullcap) as we entered the mosque in Baharak. Among his network of trading partners and relatives in the eastern part of the Wakhan, he was also fond of putting on his favorite hat of all, a dashing peacock blue fedora—an expression, I suppose, of style in the more conventional sense of the word.

Sarfraz's chameleon-like qualities included the spoken word as well as dress. His mastery of the seven languages at his command extended beyond lexicon and grammar to embrace a smorgasbord of accents and inflections. In Kabul his Dari might sound crisp and gentrified, but as soon as we were in the mountains, he would gradually downshift, like a truck descending a long grade, through a series of increasingly less refined accents and dialects until he abandoned Dari for Wakhi before finally sliding into Burushkaski—the patois of his Wakhan ancestors. (He kept his Pashto in reserve for the Pashtun-dominated territories east of Kabul, and his Urdu, Punjabi, and English for Pakistan.) Perhaps the only thing Sarfraz would not do in order to be as local as possible was to grow a beard. Other than that, he freely adopted any ruse he could conceive—including telling elaborate lies about where he was from and what he was up to—in order to fit in and avoid hitting people's trigger points.

My job was to follow his lead by copying his mannerisms and his demeanor. I would mimic the manner in which Sarfraz crossed his legs as he sat, the angle at which he held a teacup, even where he permitted his gaze to fall. Under these circumstances, of course, I wasn't deluding myself into thinking that I'd actually be mistaken for a local. But by following Sarfraz's mannerisms and body language, I was hoping to avoid giving myself away as a wealthy American interloper. The goal was simply to make anyone whom we encountered experience a moment of confusion in which they dwelled, however briefly, on the possibility that in some strange way that they didn't quite understand, I might actually belong. And as we moved around the countryside north of Kabul, this often worked surprisingly well—a tendency helped by the fact that Afghanistan is a vast melting pot in which green eyes, brown hair, and Caucasian features are not at all uncommon.

The second part of Sarfraz's kidnap-prevention strategy involved transportation, and it was here that things started to get exciting.

Moving from one destination to the next inside Pakistan was a fairly simple matter. Suleman Minhas, the CAI manager in Islamabad, ferried us around the city in a company-owned Toyota Corolla, and for the mountains of Baltistan we relied on a twenty-eight-year-old, four-wheel-drive Land Cruiser. When none of these vehicles was available, we would hire one from a pool of local Pakistani drivers whom we had known for years. Afghanistan, however, was quite different. Because we had neither a fleet of our own vehicles nor a network of trusted chauffeurs, we were usually forced to rent a car and driver on the spot, an arrangement that placed us at the mercy of people we'd never met and whose loyalties were unknown.

The process began with Sarfraz's paying a visit to a roadside bazaar in Kabul and negotiating an arrangement without actually telling anyone where we were heading. If there were a bunch of men standing around the rental place, Sarfraz might ostentatiously declare that he was looking for someone to take us to, say, Mazar-i-Sharif or Kandahar or Bamiyan—anywhere but our true destination. After he had completed his negotiations and we had piled into the vehicle, he would announce that our plans had changed, divulging as little information as possible about the "new" destination—often no more than the name of a village twenty or thirty miles up the road.

Once we were heading in the correct direction, he would begin sniffing the air for signs that something might be wrong, and if his suspicions were aroused, all bets were off. If the driver seemed to be asking too many questions or spending too much time on his cell phone or simply didn't look right, Sarfraz would abruptly exclaim that we needed to pull over at the next roadside truck stop, explain that he was dashing inside for a cup of tea, and once inside set about arranging for another car and driver. When he found someone new, he'd dash back out, open the door, and start flinging our bags into the parking lot. Then he'd toss a handful of money at the driver and tell him to get lost, and off we'd go—until it was time to fire the new driver. When it came to such precautions, he was unapologetic and completely ruthless.

Sarfraz also preferred to hire and fire drivers based on ethnicity and tribal affiliation. At any given point on the road, the goal was always to place ourselves in the hands of someone local, a man whose face and name would be known in the event that we were stopped at a roadblock or pulled over. Hiring local was also, in his view, the best way to obtain accurate information about road conditions, the weather, and the likelihood of being robbed.

This approach differed markedly from the conspicuous transport arrangements preferred by the larger humanitarian organizations and the international consulting groups, most of whom were easily distinguished by their shiny SUVs equipped with tinted windows, air-conditioning, and twelve-foot-long radio antennae. "That big antenna makes them a perfect target for the Taliban!" he would exclaim. He was also contemptuous of the disconnect that such equipment created between the employees of those organizations and the locals on whose behalf they were working.

The greatest likelihood of our being abducted or attacked was during the thirty-hour drive from Kabul to Baharak, and on this stretch of the drive, Sarfraz's concerns about security occasionally placed him at odds with my desire to get to know ordinary Afghans—a point of contention that he and I still wrestle with even today. This difference first surfaced during one of our earliest trips together in the spring of 2004.

As usual, we had left from Kabul late in the afternoon in order to pass unimpeded through the Salang Tunnel, which was only open to civilian traffic at night. Just north of the tunnel, the rattletrap jeep we had hired emitted a loud sizzle, and steam began pouring out of the engine. Sarfraz ordered the driver to drift down the hill about a mile and pull into a roadside mechanic shop. There, a boy who was no older than eleven stepped up in a pair of flip-flops to ask what we needed. His head was shaved and covered with a black woolen cap, and he wore an oil-stained *shalwar kamiz* that was coated with grease. His name was Abdul, and he walked with a limp.

Abdul jumped into the engine compartment like an acrobat, and by the time Sarfraz and I had eaten a quick meal and had a cup of tea at a nearby canteen, our young mechanic had deftly replaced our radiator and hoses. He told us the price was fourteen hundred Afghans (about twenty-eight dollars), and as Sarfraz counted out the money, I tried to get a sense of who Abdul was and what his story entailed.

"Where is your father?" I asked. "It is nearly midnight and you are working alone?"

"I am an orphan from Pul-e-Khumri," he replied matter-of-factly. "I have no father because the Taliban killed my entire family."

"Where do you live?"

"I live here—I sleep in the truck trailer over there where we keep our spare parts." He pointed to a rusting metal container.

"How much money do you make?" I asked as I searched in my pocket to offer him a small tip.

"None," he replied. "I don't get paid—I only get some food, tea, and a place to sleep. I work day and night, every day, and sleep when there is no customer. And if my boss finds out I have taken any money, he will beat me with the iron rod over there."

By this point our driver was revving the engine to signal that we needed to get moving, and Sarfraz had lit up a cigarette and was glaring at me with impatience. It was the middle of the night on a dangerous road, we were behind schedule, and it was time to go.

"Sarfraz," I pleaded, initiating an exchange that he and I were to repeat endlessly over the next several years, "can't we please do something here?"

"Greg, this is Afghanistan—you cannot help everyone!" Sarfraz barked. "If he works hard, this boy might eventually own his boss's garage. But for now he has food and a place to sleep, and that is better than half of the orphans in Afghanistan."

"Okay, but how about if we just—"

"No, Greg!" he declared, cutting me off. "I promise that when I pass through here again, I will stop to check on Abdul. But we really need to go now, or we will become *shahids* on the highway, and for that your wife will never forgive me."

Knowing that he was right, I pulled out my camera to take a picture of the boy mechanic, and then we drove away.

On his next trip north, Sarfraz did indeed stop to check on Abdul and discovered that another young boy was working in his place. Sarfraz asked what had happened to Abdul, but no one in the shop could offer any information. Perhaps he had gone north to Faizabad, or maybe south to Kabul. No one knew anything except that Abdul, whose story seemed to mirror that of so many others in this nation of orphans, had simply disappeared.

In the black-and-white image I shot that night, Abdul is standing in the garage, covered in grease and oil, with a flat expression of resignation and loss that no eleven-year-old boy should ever feel. The photo sits on my desk in Bozeman, and I see it every day that I am home.

Once we finally reached Baharak and were traveling through territory controlled by Sadhar Khan, Sarfraz's concerns about security began to drop away. They were immediately replaced, however, by a whole new set of challenges connected to the terrain.

The rutted dirt track through the western half of the Wakhan Corridor followed the Panj River, and during the spring and summer months the runoff from the glaciers and snowfields in the Hindu Kush created a series of channels that spilled directly across the roadbed. These flood zones could be up to half a mile wide, consisting mostly of loose gravel interlaced with braided streams of varying widths and depths. Upon reaching the edge of a new series of streams, we often were forced to cruise up and down the shoreline for half an hour or more before finding a spot that seemed to offer a promising place to cross. Then Sarfraz would order the driver to gun his engine and blast into the water with as much speed as possible. If we were lucky, we'd smash through to the other side. If not, we might wind up in waist-high water that would gush through the floorboards and fill up the inside of the car. Then we'd have to pile out, make our way to the edge of the stream, wait for a truck or a jeep to come by, and pay them to haul us out.

It's fair to say that Sarfraz and I treated our drivers without mercy. We goaded them into pushing their vehicles to the point where the axle seized or the transmission dropped out or the muffler was torn to pieces. If the driver himself had been forced beyond the point of exhaustion, Sarfraz would order him into the back and one of us would get behind the wheel. In the spring and the fall we'd hydroplane through acres of mud (which can be two or three feet deep in the Wakhan) until the vehicles would bog down and gurgle to a stop. Then, while the driver headed off to find a team of yaks to pull his car out, Sarfraz and I would take off our shoes, and sometimes even our pants, and start walking. (The tunic top of a *shalwar kamiz* extends well below the knees, so exposure was not a problem.)

Sooner or later, we would reach our goal—whatever stretch of the Corridor formed the focus of the trip. And it was at this point that our real work would begin.

Over the years, Sarfraz and I gradually developed a routine to which we would adhere once we had arrived in a particular "project zone." Each day would begin well before dawn, when we would wake up, blinking, in the same clothes we'd been wearing for more than a week, surrounded by the components of our mobile office: one small black backpack, a wheeled compact carry-on, and my black Pelican case bearing the THE LAST BEST PLACE bumper sticker. Together these pieces of luggage held all the paperwork for our schools in the Wakhan, along with several extra copies of *Three Cups of Tea* (which made excellent presents to the mujahadeen), our sat phone, a Nikon battery charger, one spare 28 mm camera lens, a spare *shalwar kamiz*, a Sony laptop, three cameras, several large bricks of cash, and our GPS unit.

First on the agenda were morning ablutions, which basically consisted of me smearing some aloe-scented hand sanitizer into my hair and Sarfraz scratching himself in the right spots. (Showers, bathtubs, and wet wipes were extremely scarce in the Wakhan.) Then we would pop the cap on our jumbo-size jar of ibuprofen, and each of us would take two or three tablets as a prebreakfast appetizer. (When we were going hard, we'd each go through about twelve or fifteen pills a day in order to help dull the aches and pains induced by the arduous travel and the lack of sleep.) At this point, one of us might put on the pair of reading glasses that we shared—we both have the same prescription—while the other stepped outside with the toothbrush. (Yep, we shared that, too.)

The spectacle of two men passing personal grooming items back and forth was bizarre enough that one morning a reporter from a national magazine, who was traveling with us in order to write an article about the Wakhan, asked me to provide a list of everything that Sarfraz and I used in common.

"Well, let's see," I replied. "We share our jackets, our razors, our hairbrush, our soap, our socks, our hats, our *shalwar kamiz*, our undershirts—"

"How about your underwear?" the reporter interjected. "Do you guys share that?"

"Look, I'm not sure I want to reveal this," I said, squirming with embarrassment, "but there's really no sense in lying about it either." Then I explained that having spent the first fifteen years of my childhood in rural Tanzania—where underwear is not a big priority—I have sort of gone "alpine style" for my entire life.

"And what about you, Sarfraz?" demanded the reporter, who was diligently writing all of this down.

"Alpine style for me, too."

When we had completed our morning ritual, it was time to pile back into the car, hit the road, and head off toward that day's destination. Upon arrival, the first item on the agenda called for an inspection of the school—usually surrounded by a scrum of children tugging us by the hands. (One of the greatest joys in my work is spending time with the students and teachers, and at every school, I make it a priority to greet each child, one by one, and encourage them to give me an update on how their studies are progressing.)

At every stop where there was a project, the bricks of cash that we were carrying were brought out and Sarfraz would balance the accounts with Mullah Mohammed, sixty-three, a former Taliban bookkeeper from the village of Khundud who served as our accountant for the entire Wakhan (and who usually traveled with us). Our ledgers were kept according to the old British double-entry system and were laid out by hand, from right to left, in Persian script. Every transaction was recorded down to the penny, and at the end of each accounting session, which could take hours, Sarfraz would "seal" the ledger by drawing a line in ink along the edge of the page so that no additional expenses could be written in later. Then he would solemnly warn Mullah Mohammed that if any errors later emerged, Mullah Mohammed would be shipped off to rejoin the Taliban.

While this business unfolded, I often found myself besieged by people submitting requests for assistance. In Khundud, there might be a man asking for money to set up a grocery store in exchange for providing tutoring services to our students. In the town of Ishkoshem, I might be approached by a pair of local officials seeking funds for a water-delivery system. In the tiny hamlet of Piggush, the school principal might claim to need additional cash to purchase desks and filing cabinets for her teachers. The pleading was always polite, but the needs were endless: more books, more pencils, more uniforms, another classroom. I would get proposal after proposal, and unfortunately, I would have to say no to dozens of them, even though many of the petitioners might have traveled for days on foot or by public transport to present me with their requests.

As the day progressed, Sarfraz and I would also find ourselves passing the sat phone back and forth in order to keep in contact with the rest of the CAI staff who were scattered throughout the Punjab, Baltistan, and eastern Afghanistan. There were hourly chats with Suleman in Islamabad, who served as our communications hub and who would keep me abreast of who among the staff was arguing with whom—an inevitable by-product of an organization staffed with members of half a dozen different tribal and religious backgrounds.

Finally, as evening drew near, we would be invited to gather at the home of a village leader and convene with the local heavyweights for a *jirga,* or council session. A *jirga* is a formal gathering of elders sitting in a circle on a carpet, or under a tree, and as a rule the participants are forbidden from adjourning until consensus has been achieved around a decision. As a result, *jirgas* can go on for hours and often extend through much of the night. They invariably feature long speeches, periods of intense deliberation conducted in absolute silence, and prodigious amounts of tea drinking.

Toward dawn, Sarfraz and I would snatch a brief nap in an empty room in someone's house or bunk down on the floor of the school. Two or three hours later, it would be time to pack up, pile into our hired vehicle, and race off to the next project. And so it would go, school by school and village by village, until we had worked our way through the places we needed to visit and it was time for me to fly home to Montana and for Sarfraz to head back to the Charpurson Valley.

These trips were long and grueling, and during the course of them my respect and affection for Sarfraz continued to deepen. By the end of that first year, he had impressed me with his intelligence, his diligence, and his work ethic. He was culturally savvy, constantly on the move, and able to switch between charming and harsh as the situation demanded. For our point man in the

Wakhan, I do not think there could have been a better choice than Sarfraz Khan.

There was one area, however, in which both he and I were an absolute disaster.

Thanks to Sadhar Khan's support and protection, we were making fair progress inside the Wakhan itself. Eventually, however, we would need to make contact with the government in Kabul and obtain official permission for our projects. With this in mind, Sarfraz and I set up meetings with a number of government officials during the course of three separate visits to the capital city—and it was in those offices that we achieved a whole new level of *no much success*.

To be fair to the officials with whom we collided, the country they were attempting to govern had been at war for more than two decades, and virtually every aspect of civil society was in shambles. Nevertheless, the people we tried to work with in Kabul didn't make it easy for us to help them rebuild their own school system. On the contrary, I'd say. Never have we drunk three cups of tea so many times to so little purpose.

In that part of the world, if an office doesn't have its own tea, someone has to go for takeout, which can sometimes take up to half an hour. As often as not, we would wait for the tea and only after it had arrived be informed that the individual we needed to see wasn't in. Once or twice, we announced the name of the official we needed to see and were told "no problem," invited for tea, eventually served, and then informed that this person wasn't actually in the office after all, and could we come back tomorrow? To some degree you get used to this in central Asia, but in Kabul such tendencies were more pronounced than usual.

During one of our first meetings, we ran into trouble at the offices of the Interior Ministry, to which we had been shuttled from the Education Ministry. Interior occupied a decrepit multistory building in downtown Kabul, and the guards at the entrance and in the hallways were all armed with AK-47s. We trudged up the stairs to the reception area on the second floor, where I told the young man behind the desk that I had with me letters from the education officials in Badakshan Province stipulating that the Central Asia Institute had received approval to build schools inside the Wakhan Corridor. We had confirmed our appointment in advance by phone, and all we needed were the proper federal certificates.

"You have arrived unannounced," declared the official after running his finger down the day's list of appointments and failing to find our names. "And now you are asking us to give you permission to build some schools? Who instructed you to come here?"

"Well, our letters are from the authorities at the village, district, and provincial level," we explained. "But now we need federal approval, and that's why we're here to see you."

"But why are you proposing to build schools in the Wakhan?" he exclaimed. "We already have hundreds of schools there! Why don't you instead propose to build some schools in Kabul or Kandahar—for that I would be happy to give you permission."

"But there is not a single school in the eastern half of the Wakhan Corridor," I responded.

"That is not true!" he said.

At this point, Sarfraz unfurled a map and began pointing out the places in the Wakhan that needed schools.

"But this is not even part of Afghanistan!" the man cried. "Why are you proposing to build schools in China?"

"The fact of the matter, sir," said Sarfraz, "is that this is *your* country."

"Well, even if it *is* Afghanistan," he continued, "schools are not necessary in this area because no one lives there."

Within the span of a single five-minute exchange, this official had asserted that the Wakhan was filled with hundreds of schools, that the Wakhan was not part of Afghanistan, and that no one actually lived in the Wakhan.

Needless to say, we left that office empty-handed.

In the following months, our exchanges with members of the various government ministries to which we were dispatched were equally fruitless. That was the norm in Kabul. Out in the countryside, the main concern of the education directors, the *commandhans,* and the local religious leaders who had already provided us with stamped and signed authorizations was that we continue with our work. And yet, by the beginning of 2005, we had failed even to register as an officially approved NGO working in Afghanistan, much less to receive retroactive permission for the schools that we had already started constructing.

As Sarfraz would say, "paper side" was never our strong suit.

On the "project side," however, we were doing reasonably well. By now, Sarfraz and I had launched five projects in the Wakhan, with another dozen in the works. There was much to be pleased about—yet one concern continued to prod at the back of my mind. There was still the matter of the unfulfilled promise that I had made to the Kirghiz concerning the most remote school of all.

CHAPTER 6

The Seal of the Kirghiz Khan

*But I know, somehow, that only
when it is dark enough, can you see the stars.*
—MARTIN LUTHER KING JR.

Teacher in Afghanistan

PHOTO: © 2009 TERU KUWAYAMA

*A*s I have mentioned, the construction of Sadhar Khan's school had started in 2004. The general contractor was Haji Baba, the mujahadeen who claimed the honor of having taken out a Soviet helicopter in Badakshan with a Stinger missile. Under his supervision, the foundation, walls, roof, and interior framing were completed by winter. When the snow began to melt, his crews raced to complete everything else—the finishing carpentry in the classrooms, the latrines, the kerosene stove heaters, and the boundary wall. By spring, the little white schoolhouse with the lime green trim in the village of Yardar was the pride of the entire valley and was almost ready to open its doors to its first class of 358 students. Just as Sadhar Khan had promised, more than two hundred of them were girls, including two of his own daughters.

In early May, I arrived in Kabul and caught a UN flight into Faizabad, where Sadhar Khan's oldest son, Waris, met me in his Soviet-era jeep and shuttled me to Baharak, where Sadhar Khan was waiting to take me on a tour of the new school. With only twelve classrooms, it was hardly our biggest or most elaborate project. But even so, I had to admit that it was a real beauty. Its most impressive feature was the intricate stonework, chiseled and carved from the blasted boulders in the mountains. It was clear that Sadhar Khan was enormously pleased and proud, and together we basked in a sense of accomplishment over this, the very first school we had built in Badakshan.

During the coming week, Waris was planning to enlist the help of several men in the surrounding community to build the desks and chairs—a smart move that would avoid the high cost of purchasing the furniture from Kabul and paying the exorbitant shipping costs. In the meantime, my plan was to head into the Wakhan and meet up with Sarfraz so that we could attend the inauguration of our school in the village of Sarhad. If everything went as planned, I'd be able to toast the opening of the projects on either end of our two-pronged "literary pincer movement."

A day later, traveling with a jeep and driver provided by Sadhar Khan, I arrived in Sarhad. It was a gorgeous morning—the sky was a soft robin's-egg blue and the shadows of swiftly moving clouds were playing across the lemon yellow contours of the enormous peaks that rise abruptly to the north and south of Sarhad. Sarfraz and I rode to witness the opening day of school by squatting in a wooden trailer pulled by a red tractor. The lurching and bumping was so violent that we had to brace ourselves against the sides of the trailer to avoid being pitched out.

The stone-walled school had been constructed in the shape of a circle, a local design, and it boasted nine classrooms with a sunroof that would permit streaming sunlight to illuminate the interior while providing warmth. Waiting in the courtyard were 220 eager students and their teachers. The girls were clad in traditional crimson tribal dresses with woolen stockings wrapped around their legs, while the boys wore the drab, gray *shalwar kamiz* that is standard attire in the region.

As often happens at such events, the kids were just beside themselves with anticipation. As Sarfraz and I hopped out of the trailer, they gathered in a line to welcome us. One of the students at the front of the line, a wispy third grader named Aisha, displayed the knock-kneed gait that is a by-product of rickets, an ailment common to the remote interior of the Wakhan, where the diet is deficient in vitamin D. Unlike most of the girls, who shyly greeted me with a traditional kiss to the back of my outstretched hand, Aisha gave me an enormous hug and refused to let go.

The entrance to the school's interior compound was guarded by a pair of myrtle green metal gates, and the honor of taking the first official steps inside was given to a group of the village's most respected elders, all of them men. Then one by one, the children gingerly stepped through. Some were clad in rubber boots, others wore sandals, and several were in their bare feet. All of them were closely watched by Tashi Boi, the village chief, who recited the name of each child as he or she walked through the gate and gave a crisp nod of approval.

As I watched the children step into the school courtyard, I couldn't help but notice that the gray, lunar-looking dust now bore the imprints of a mosaic of footprints, and I was reminded, oddly enough, of the moment when Neil Armstrong had stepped onto the surface of the moon. *One small step for a brave young girl,* I thought as the knock-kneed Aisha tottered into the courtyard, *one giant leap for this community.*

Standing beside me was Doug Chabot, the husband of Genevieve, CAI's international program manager, who has volunteered to help us over the years and who had arrived a few days earlier with Sarfraz. "This is really something to watch," murmured Doug, turning to me with a look of subdued amazement that suggested that he was beginning to fathom what the promise of education meant to a village like Sarhad. "They are just *hungry* for this, aren't they?"

I nodded silently and could not help but think back to the afternoon in 2002 when Afghanistan's minister of finance had told me that "the last thing the people in the remote areas want is schools."

The following morning, I bade farewell to Sarfraz and, together with Mullah Mohammed, the CAI's ex-Taliban bookkeeper, began heading back to Baharak. By this point, word of our arrival had spread throughout the Corridor, and as we bounced along the rutted jeep track, we were unable to travel more than a couple of miles without encountering a cluster of people waiting by the side of the road to flag down our vehicle and invite us inside for a cup of tea so that they could submit a special request.

The message was always the same: We have heard about the *maktab* (school) that you have just opened in Sarhad, and we know that you plan to build new schools next year in Wargeant, Babu Tengi, and Pikui. What about us? Will you not consider helping our children by building a *maktab* for them, too? With all the stopping and starting, it took more than forty-eight hours before we made it back to Baharak and somewhere along that stretch of road, the outside world caught up with us.

Several days earlier, *Newsweek* magazine had published an article that suggested that an American soldier stationed at the U.S. prison in Guantánamo Bay had taken a copy of the Koran and flushed it down a toilet. The editors would soon retract the story, but the damage had already been done, and as word of this alleged desecration reverberated throughout the Muslim world, events quickly began spinning out of control.

In Afghanistan, the first riots took place in Jalalabad on Wednesday, May 11. At about 10:00 P.M. that night, Mullah Mohammed and I arrived in Baharak. After driving to Sadhar Khan's home and being informed that he was not there, we headed into the center of town with the intention of spending the night on the floor of a crowded public "guesthouse." On the way there, however, I was approached by a guard who worked for Wohid Khan, a former mujahadeen commander and a colleague of Sadhar Khan's who is in charge of the Border Security Force in eastern Badakshan. After warning us that trouble was brewing in town, the guard urged Mullah Mohammed and me to proceed to a building owned by Wohid Khan, where we could join a group of travelers who were spending the night under his protection.

Happy to comply, we headed over to the two-story apartment building, where a cluster of perhaps twenty Afghans had gathered. By now it was nearly midnight, and just as we were preparing for bed, in strode Wohid Khan. In a typical demonstration of Afghan hospitality, he insisted on feeding everyone dinner. We all filed into another room and sat cross-legged on Persian rugs while platters of roast lamb and Kabuli rice were served.

I found myself sitting next to two dignified but ragged figures with Mongolian features. The gentleman to my immediate left, who was wearing thick eyeglasses and a black robe made of dense cloth, looked to be about seventy years old. He politely introduced himself as Niaz Ali and explained that he was the imam, or spiritual leader, of a group of Kirghiz nomads who lived in the High Pamir, at the far eastern end of the Wakhan.

My pleasure at making Niaz Ali's acquaintance was quickly overtaken by a sense of astonishment and delight when he introduced me to his companion, who was sitting to my right—a dusty, disheveled elder clad in corduroy breeches and high leather boots who was draped in the exhausted demeanor of a man who had been on the road far longer than he might have wished. This was none other than Abdul Rashid Khan, the very man who had sent his son, Roshan, over the Irshad Pass to find me in the fall of 1999.

It was an extraordinary coincidence. Here in Baharak, Abdul Rashid Khan and I had finally been brought together around a plate of roast lamb, long after midnight on the eve of a full-blown religious riot. But even more remarkable, as I was about to discover, were the events that had drawn this man from his home in the mountains at the far end of the Wakhan. As we tucked into the food laid before us, he told me the story of the arduous journey he had just completed to meet the president of Afghanistan in Kabul, and the reasons why he was now returning, empty-handed and nearly broke, to his people in the High Pamir.

During the mid-1990s, the Afghan forces that had defeated the Soviet army found themselves grappling with the impossible challenge of rebuilding a war-shattered nation without any significant assistance from their former allies abroad, including the United States. In the absence of outside aid, one of the few reliable sources of wealth was opium—a crop that had offered a lucrative source of income to a number of cash-strapped mujahadeen commanders during the Soviet occupation. By the early 1990s, so much heroin was flowing out of the country that Afghanistan rivaled Southeast Asia as the prime source of the world's opium supply. Then in 1994, as one province and city after another fell to the armies of Mullah Omar, many members of Badakshan's beleaguered mujahadeen found themselves turning to drug dealing as their primary means of financing their war against the Taliban, sending enormous quantities north through new overland routes developed by organized crime groups in Russia, who would transport it to Moscow and European cities beyond.

In addition to taxing the growth and export of opium from within their own territory, these mujahadeen had also played a role in selling drugs to peasants in remote villages, especially the Wakhi and Kirghiz of the Wakhan. In village after village, the pattern repeated itself: Within the tight confines of a close-knit household, addiction would spread from an ailing husband or a rebellious teenager to every member of the family, including the women, the elderly, and even toddlers. From there the scourge would spread to members of the extended community, enveloping entire villages. Starting in the late 1990s, Ismaili and Kirghiz communities all across the Corridor began reporting opium addicts in every stratum of society, with estimates as high as a quarter of the entire adult population.

The results were devastating. Families suffering from advanced levels of addiction wound up selling everything they owned to finance their three-times-a-day habit. First to go were their possessions—mainly the goats, sheep, and yaks—followed by their land, and in the most extreme circumstances, even their daughters, who came to be known as opium brides. (It is not uncommon to find entire families sold into servitude.) Those who remained were reduced to a diet of tea and bread, making them vulnerable to sickness and diseases.

By early 2005, things had become so desperate that Abdul Rashid Khan decided to form a delegation of leaders from northeastern Afghanistan and travel to Kabul to lay these grievances before the newly elected president, Hamid Karzai. In addition to making Karzai aware of the problems stemming from heroin addiction, the representatives intended to present evidence that their sector of the country lacked virtually any semblance of a functioning federal government.

For Abdul Rashid Khan, the trip to the capital took an entire month and involved traveling by horse, jeep, and public transport. Upon reaching Kabul in early March, he and Niaz Ali spent several weeks moving around various government ministries in an effort to meet with officials who were responsible for services such as education, transportation, health care, and post offices. During these encounters, they got the same kind of runaround that Sarfraz and I had met with during our own visits. Meanwhile, they set themselves up in a rundown apartment with no heat or electricity and petitioned for an audience with President Karzai. They waited two months before receiving a reply.

When they were finally granted an audience, the president permitted Abdul Rashid Khan to get halfway through his itemization of the problems among his people before cutting him off. "Don't worry," Karzai interrupted. "I am going to arrange food—I will send you back with food on helicopters. You will not go home without a solution to your problems. We will arrange what documentation is needed for the clinics, and we will get your food."

With that, the meeting was over.

There was no follow-up from Karzai's office on the matters of food, helicopters, medical services, or anything else. In early May, Abdul Rashid Khan and Niaz Ali realized that the president's promises were not going to be fulfilled and started their journey home to the Wakhan empty-handed—and by road.

By the time Abdul Rashid Khan and I met at Wohid Khan's supper in Baharak, the two Kirghiz leaders had been away from home for more than four months and had squandered much of their personal fortune. Upon reaching the Pamirs, they would be faced with the duty of informing their people that it had all been for naught.

When he had finished relating this tale, Abdul Rashid Khan confirmed that he knew all about my meeting with his son at the entrance to the Irshad Pass and expressed his amazement that we were now, on the heels of his brutally disappointing sojourn in Kabul, finally meeting for the first time. It was a very emotional exchange: He declared that he was deeply honored to meet me; I protested that it was a far greater honor to meet *him*. Then the *duas* began to flow from his hands, one after the other, and he and Niaz Ali began a Koranic recitation out of sheer joy.

A *dua* is a prayer invoked as a blessing or thanks to Allah, and in the case of Abdul Rashid Khan's invocation, it was partly an expression of gratitude over the miracle that we had finally met and partly an expression of his hope that the humiliating and fruitless quest on which he had embarked might actually result in something positive.

"All I really want for my people is a school so that we can provide education for our children," he said. "To achieve that, I am willing to give up all of my wealth—all of my sheep, all of my camels, all of my yaks—everything I have, if only Allah will grant this one request."

"But you have nothing to worry about," I said. "I have already promised your son that we will build you a school."

"If that is truly the case," he replied, "then let us start now—this very minute!"

Ooba (yes), I told Abdul Rashid Khan, but first I have to call someone. I stepped into the cool evening outside, turned on my sat phone, and punched the number for Karen McCown, one of our directors, who lives in the Bay Area. Seeking permission from our board to fund a particular school is not the way we normally do things at the CAI. But I was excited and overwhelmed, and so was everyone else, and the emotions of the moment took over.

"Karen," I blurted, "do you remember the Kirghiz tribesmen who rode across the border and found me in Zuudkhan in October of 1999? Well, I am finally here with Abdul Rashid Khan, and he is in desperate straits, and we have to start the school for him and his people."

My excitement was apparently contagious, even over the phone.

"Go ahead, Greg," Karen declared. "I'll check with the board and get retroactive approval, but let's get this show on the road!"

When I returned to the dining room and announced that we had the funding for the school, Abdul Rashid Khan declared that he wanted to draw up a formal agreement right then and there. As the leader of the Kirghiz, it was his duty to provide a guarantee that his people would donate the land and the labor in order to ensure that this project would go forward.

Wohid Khan summoned a guard to give me a spiral notebook and a pen, and I drew up a standard CAI contract, the document that codifies our arrangement with any new community. I then handed the paper to Niaz Ali and he transcribed it into Kirghiz with a vintage fountain pen. It was only eight sentences long, and in English it read as follows:

> *Bismillah ir-Rahman ir-Rahim*
>
> *In the name of Allah, the Merciful, the Beneficial*
>
> *With the witness of Commandhan Wohid Khan, Abdul Rashid Khan, Mullah Mohammed, and Greg Mortenson*
>
> *Whereas, the Kirghiz people of the Wakhan have no school, teacher, or education*
>
> *And Whereas, the Afghanistan government has not provided us schools as promised*
>
> *The Kirghiz people, under the leadership of Abdul Rashid Khan, hereby sign this agreement to build a four-room school at Bozai Gumbaz, Wakhan, with the assistance of registered charity NGO Central Asia Institute.*
>
> *Central Asia Institute will provide building materials, skilled labor, school supplies, and help with teachers' salary and training*

Abdul Rashid Khan agrees to provide free land, subsidized manual labor, and support for teachers.

The exact terms of the budget and agreement will be worked out after a jirga is convened in Bozoi Gumbaz.

Abdul Rashid Khan

Wohid Khan

Greg Mortenson

Mullah Mohammed

Then Abdul Rashid Khan did something that I had never seen. He reached inside his jacket and pulled out a tiny brown leather satchel. Inside was a very old wooden stamp with the official seal of the Khan of the Kirghiz of the Little Pamir. On this seal was emblazoned a pair of Marco Polo sheep horns, twisted in a spiral. He also had an ink dipper, and with this he carefully blotted ink onto the stamp, which I noticed had a tiny crack running down the middle, then placed this mark upon the contract. When he was through, he took a red candle, dribbled a small circle of wax at the bottom of the stamped seal, and with ponderous gravity, pressed his thumbprint into the wax.

When this formality was complete, Niaz Ali launched into a lengthy prayer that apparently included half of Kirghiz history and that petitioned, among many other things, that

Allah the Compassionate, Allah the Merciful, Allah the Beneficent, might watch over Wohid Khan, whose food had brought these humble servants of Islam together for this miraculous meeting . . . and the men of the eastern Badakshan border security force, who were protecting

us on this most dangerous night ... and, yes, even
President Hamid Karzai, who may not have kept his
promise but who bore the weight of a shattered nation
on his shoulders, which surely is a greater burden than
any man ever should be called upon to bear ... and
this school-building American mountaineer, who is
attempting to honor the first word of the Holy Koran,
Ikra ("to read") by lighting a lamp for the illiterate
daughters of Islam ... and this American's strange band
of employees—first of all, bless the Sunnis among them,
of course, but the Shiites, too; and yes, even this crazy
Ismaili from Pakistan with the broken hand named
Sarfraz Khan ... may Allah shower his blessings upon
them all ...

Praise be to God ...
There is no God but God ...
And Muhammad is His Prophet ...
La Ilaha Illa-Allah ...

This went on for quite some time. When it was finally over, everyone clapped. Abdul Rashid Khan and I embraced. And then Wohid Khan solemnly declared that if it became necessary, he would personally travel to Kabul to ensure that no corrupt bureaucrat or misguided government official dared to interfere with the construction of this school for the Kirghiz of the Little Pamir.

Thus ended one of the most memorable encounters I have experienced during the twelve years since I failed to climb K2 and wound up stumbling into the village of Korphe. It was remarkable on its own terms, to be sure—but it was rendered even more astonishing, it now seems to me, by virtue of the events that were about to unfold.

At about ten o'clock the following morning, Mullah Mohammed and I bade farewell to our Kirghiz friends and left Baharak, heading west for Faizabad. It was now Friday the thirteenth, and as we made our way through town we could see that a large group of men had gathered around the Najmuddin Khan Wosiq mosque, which was located just off the bazaar. They looked angry, and many of them were carrying hoes, shovels, and sticks.

We kept driving, reached Faizabad about three hours later, and immediately checked into the Marco Polo Club, a former Soviet guesthouse on an island in the middle of the roaring Amu Darya River that currently functions as a decrepit hotel. By now, the *Newsweek* story about the desecration of the Koran had filtered into every corner of the Muslim world, and enraged imams from Morocco to Islamabad were preparing to launch fiery sermons on the subject during Friday prayers, which typically begin around 1:30 P.M. Fearing that things might get out of hand, the employees of almost every foreign NGO in eastern Badakshan appeared to be evacuating Faizabad, either by getting a seat on the one UN flight at the airport or by heading south on the road to Kabul in their Land Cruisers.

My thinking in these matters has always been different. When things get tense, I'd rather be with local people than with foreigners, even if the foreigners have guns. So I stayed put at the Marco Polo.

That evening, a group of aid workers who were fleeing from Baharak to Kabul stopped in Faizabad and brought word that a pair of conservative mullahs had given especially inflammatory speeches that afternoon at the Baharak mosque in which they had declared that the insult to the Koran that had taken place at Guantánamo Bay was an unpardonable offense that needed to be met with violence. In response, several hundred men had swarmed out of the mosque into the streets of Baharak and headed southeast toward a street that houses the offices of nearly every foreign aid agency in town.

During the next several hours of rioting, each of these offices was ransacked. The windows were smashed, the doors broken down. While every piece of furniture and equipment inside was destroyed, the vehicles parked outside them were pummeled with sledgehammers and crowbars, then set on fire. In the process, four local residents who had been employed by these organizations were murdered and the entire bazaar was smashed to pieces. Wohid Khan and the Border Security Force were eventually able to restore order and quell the violence, but only after shooting down two rioters, wounding at least a dozen more, and arresting more than fifty.

When word of these events reached me in Faizabad, my heart sank. Under most circumstances, I remain optimistic that things will work out for us in Asia, but on that evening, I was convinced that our new school just outside Baharak, which is less than a mile from the street where the NGO offices were attacked, had been gutted and destroyed. If that had indeed happened, it would be a setback for our entire Wakhan initiative, one from which we might not recover. Years of work and patient negotiation might spiral down the drain, along with our newly lit hopes of finally making good on our promise to Abdul Rashid Khan and his people in the Pamirs. In short, if this new school in the backyard of our strongest supporter in the entire province—Sadhar Khan himself—had been sacked by the mob, we could be out of business in the Wakhan.

I had no confirmation that this had actually taken place, of course, but my fears were getting the best of me. Not helping my frame of mind was Mullah Mohammed, who at some point that Friday had bolted from the Marco Polo and gone into hiding, apparently concluding that he'd be safer without me. I wasn't angry—who could blame him? But his actions seemed to underscore the extent to which everything was spinning out of control.

Two days later, Mullah Mohammed reappeared at the Marco Polo Club, apologizing profusely for having abandoned me. I wanted to ask him why he had violated the most sacrosanct of tribal codes and deserted me, but I noticed he was still terrified, literally trembling, and I reassured him we both were quite fine—but I added that we needed to line up some transportation and head for Baharak, where by now the rioting had subsided, in order to find out what had happened to our school. He quickly found a minivan for hire, and we were off.

As we drove into the outskirts of Faizabad, I began to see piles of burned wood, twisted rebar, and other remnants of the rioting piled at the north end of town. Near the main mosque, a firebombed Land Cruiser still smoldered and was missing its big antenna. Nervous men and curiosity seekers lingered on all sides of the locked-down bazaar stalls. A few local chai stands were doing a brisk business, with men congregating around them to sort out fact from fiction among the rumors that were flying through town.

Beyond Faizabad itself, there was no evidence of rioting or destruction on the sides of the roads. The farmers were in their fields weeding and rerouting irrigation channels; the small shops along the road were mostly open for business. For lunch we stopped at a local tandoori shop to get warm chai and fresh naan, hot out of a clay oven. The baker there complained that most of the vehicles that day were in a hurry to get out of the area and raced by his stand without stopping. He was amused when we told him where we were headed.

"You two are fools to be headed for Baharak today," he declared. "You should be going the other way."

Just before the entrance to Baharak, the road sweeps over a plateau and offers a stunning view of the town with the distant Hindu Kush in the south. As we topped the rise, we failed to spot anything unusual—but upon crossing the final bridge into Baharak and entering the main bazaar where the mosque and the government offices are located, it seemed as if we were passing into a war zone. Rubber tires still smoldered in the streets, which were covered with sticks, bricks, and stones.

In the middle of the bazaar, where the NGO offices began, there were gutted Land Cruisers, smashed computers, and broken glass everywhere. The mob's fury had clearly been directed at these buildings, which housed the Aga Khan Development Network, FOCUS, East West Foundation, Afghan Aid, and other NGOs. Their offices lay in ruins, and even the safes and desks had been smashed to pieces.

As we made our way down past the south end of the bazaar toward Yardar, I was braced for the worst. But when we pulled up in front of the boundary wall of the new school, I could hardly believe my eyes. No windows were broken. The door was intact. The fresh coat of lime green paint that the building had received only a week earlier was as bright as a newly minted dime.

"*Allah Akbar,*" mumbled Mullah Mohammed, and cracked a smile.

As we stood surveying the building, Sadhar Khan's son Waris walked up and explained that during the peak of the riots, a faction of the mob that was attacking the bazaar had stormed down the road in the direction of the school. Before reaching the boundary wall, however, they had been met by a group of elders who had donated the land for the school, organized the laborers who had built it, and participated in the laying of the cornerstone. These elders, or *pirs,* informed the rioters that the Central hundred students were packed in like sardines. These were the fourth, fifth, and sixth graders, and according to the two women who were teaching them, they were doing extremely well— although it might have been helpful to have some books, some paper, and some pencils.

This was my introduction to the education system serving the region of Simdara, an area with a population of roughly 4,000 people. For more than two decades, the district had been attempting to keep its schools running without any assistance whatsoever. The students had neither books nor school supplies nor uniforms, and the teachers had not been paid in more than two years—although they had been receiving weekly rations of flour in compensation for their services.

We were forced to get back on the road and catch our plane, but later I telephoned Sarfraz and asked him to look into this situation with the education office in Faizabad. The officials in Faizabad, which is less than forty miles down the road, said they had never even heard of the Simdara school district—but they would be delighted if we would consider putting in a proper school for the valley.

By this point we had committed most of our current funding in Afghanistan to the new schools inside the Wakhan, but we did manage to scrape together enough cash to begin paying the salaries of the Simdara teachers. Our hope was that within a few months, we might be able to figure out a way to get the students out of the toilet and the tents and into a structure that at least vaguely resembled an actual school.

By the time autumn arrived, however, the world had shifted on its axis, and the lives of Sarfraz, me, and the other members of the Dirty Dozen had been swept up in—and consumed by—the disaster that took place on the morning of October 8, 2005.

PART II

Qayamat

("The Apocalypse")

CHAPTER 7

A Dark and Distant Roar

On October 7, I was Prime Minister of Azad Jammu & Kashmir.
On October 8, I was Prime Minister of a graveyard.
—Sardar Sikandar Hayat Khan

Widow in refugee camp after Pakistan earthquake

One hundred and fifty million years ago, the landmass of India belonged to a supercontinent known as Gondwana that splayed across much of the southern hemipshere and was bounded by a primordial ocean called the Tethys Sea. Sometime between the Jurassic and the Late Cretaceous periods, Gondwana started breaking apart, and this geologic partition cast loose India's moorings and sent it plowing northward through the sea like an immense terrestrial barge until it rammed into the southern edge of Eurasia. The impact generated plate-tectonic forces powerful enough to crush and contort the bottom of the Tethys Sea, then thrust the entire ocean bed high into the sky. The result was a soaring arc of snow-draped peaks that now stretches for more than 1,500 miles, from the lunar-looking escarpments of eastern Afghanistan to the dripping, flower-draped forests of Bhutan.

Today, the fossilized skeletons of the trilobites, crinoids, and other marine creatures that were once suspended in the warm currents of the Tethys Sea can be found littering the summits of the Himalayas, which continue to rise at a rate of ten meters each century as the Indian subcontinent sustains its slow-motion crash into central Asia. At irregular intervals, the stresses and pressures generated by this concussion cause earthquakes to ripple across the axis of the Himalayas, one of the most active fault zones in the world. Most of these temblors are minor events that scarcely draw notice. Every few decades, however, the earth's crust is seized by a cataclysmic convulsion that sets the greatest peaks on the planet to shaking like the branches of an apple tree in a strong wind.

This is what took place in northeastern Pakistan around 8:50 A.M. on the morning of Saturday, October 8, 2005.

Because it was still Ramadan, the ninth month of the Islamic calendar, when devout Muslims are forbidden to eat or drink between sunrise and sunset, many adults were inside their homes that morning, doing chores or napping after their predawn meal. Saturday is also a school day in Pakistan, however, so most schoolchildren had already gathered inside their classrooms by the time the quake struck.

The seismic shock wave originated more than sixteen miles beneath the surface, deep under Kashmir's Neelum Valley at a point whose surface coordinates corresponded almost exactly with the Government Boys' Degree High School in the village of Patika, about twelve miles northeast of the city of Muzaffarabad. The school was a two-story brick structure, and at 8:30 A.M., eighty-one tenth-grade boys had assembled at their desks in room number six. Their first class was an English lesson conducted by a twenty-four-year-old teacher named Shaukat Ali Chaudry, a former Kashmiri guerrilla fighter and an ex-member of the Taliban whose past was as convoluted as the geography of Kashmir.

Shaukat Ali was born in Patika in 1981, and at the age of twelve, when his father died, he was forced to complete his own studies while simultaneously working as a private tutor to support his mother and his eight younger siblings. His home lay just beyond the twenty-mile range of India's Swedish-manufactured Bofors artillery cannons, but throughout his teenage years he could hear periodic Indian bombardments of nearby villages in the Neelum Valley. It was during this period, in the late 1990s, that he found himself drawn into Kashmir's burgeoning independence movement—a campaign that drew inspiration from the Afghan mujahadeen's victory over the Soviets in 1989. Not long after his sixteenth birthday, Shaukat Ali joined the Jammu Kashmir Liberation Front (JKLF), where he received guerrilla training before being assigned to quick forays to raid Indian army convoys inside the portion of Kashmir that was controlled by the Indian government.

Around this time he also made the first of several trips to Kabul to observe the Taliban's efforts to impose strict Islamic law in Afghanistan, and from there he was able to roam across portions of central Asia and Chechnya. He initially found himself impressed by the Taliban's ideological fervor and decided to join the movement, but later grew deeply troubled by the Taliban's many atrocities against civilians, and especially by their attitude toward women. Thanks to his command of Arabic—a skill that many of his illiterate fellow militants did not possess—Shaukat Ali understood that they were violating the teachings of the Koran and did not hesitate to tell them so. "If that woman was your mother or your sister," he would demand, pointing to a woman who was being persecuted by one of his colleagues, "would you dare to beat or kill her in the name of Islam?"

Torn between his relationship with a group of men who were committing crimes in the name of Islam and his longing to return to his duties as a teacher, he eventually sided with the latter. "One of the happiest days of my life," he once told me, "was when I finally put down my gun forever and took up the pen. This is the jihad that is Allah's calling for me."

He took a job at the Government Boys' Degree High School in Patika, where he also joined the faculty of the Gundi Piran Higher Secondary School for Girls, an eighth of a mile down the road, tutoring three hundred female students in English, economics, and mathematics—the first man in the history of the district permitted to teach girls. Sporting round, gold-rimmed glasses and a long black beard, he looked like a cross between an Afghan mujahadeen and a Berkeley philosophy professor. And by the fall of 2005, this young, earnest, and talented Islamic rebel was passionately devoted to empowering Kashmir's first generation of science-educated girls to enter college and eventually move into the workforce.

On the morning of October 8, Shaukat Ali's lesson plan called for him to read a passage to his English class that began with the sentence, "Sports and games are very important for physical health." Before he started reading, he looked up and spotted a student named Tarik, who had been absent the previous day.

"Tarik," he demanded, "where were you yesterday?"

Tarik shot to his feet.

"Sir, I was sick and unable to come," he explained. "Would you please repeat yesterday's lesson?"

Before Shaukat Ali could respond, a dark roar engulfed the entire Neelum Valley and the walls of the school building began to shake violently.

"Run!" cried Shaukat Ali.

He held the door tightly as the boys threaded through one by one, then followed after them while reciting the words of the First *Kalima*, one of the five pillars of the Islamic declaration of faith—*La ilaha illal-Lah, Muhammadun rasulula-Lah.* "There is no god but Allah, and Muhammed is his Prophet."

Teacher and students raced along the hall and down the stairs to join the rest of the school in the courtyard, where everyone watched in disbelief as the walls supporting the second story crumbled and the top floor of the building fell apart. Shaukat Ali and his colleagues immediately started counting heads to determine if anyone had been left behind and quickly realized that the headmaster, Akbar Ahwan, and the history teacher, Professor Khalid Husmani, were nowhere to be seen. The two men were later found dead in the rubble, along with the body of Khoshnood Ali Khan, the school clerk, who apparently had been checking the classrooms to make sure the students had all evacuated before attempting to flee himself.

It was during the brief interlude required to complete this initial roll call that several things happened. Roughly 450 miles to the southeast, tremors caused panic in the streets of the Indian cities of Amritsar and Delhi, while in the district of Poonch, the two-hundred-year-old Moti Mahal fort abruptly collapsed. Far off to the northwest, a wall in the Afghan city of Jalalabad tumbled onto a young girl, who became one of the quake's only two casualties inside Afghanistan. Meanwhile, fifty-five miles southwest in Islamabad's Blue Area, the Margalla Towers residential apartment building disintegrated, killing seventy-four people according to the Associated Press. None of those events, however, could compete with the carnage and destruction that greeted the teachers of Shaukat Ali's school when, upon completing their head count, they looked up to survey their surroundings.

Along the hills beyond the town, landslides had severed every road and buried entire villages. The bridge across the Neelum River had twisted sideways. In Patika itself, there was barely a house, *dukan* (shop), or office left standing, and people were running through the streets, many of them screaming and covered with blood.

Shaukat Ali started to rush across to the town bazaar but was brought up short when his gaze turned toward the Gundi Piran Higher Secondary School for Girls, where all that was left was pile of gray and white rubble. The entire structure had failed, trapping three hundred girls inside. Many were already dead, but some were still alive, and when the parents of these students beganing running into the schoolyard, they were greeted by the muffled cries of their daughters coming from under the wreckage.

Shaukat Ali's own home in the village of Batangi was eight miles away, and as the head of his household, he knew that his family would be looking to him for leadership in this moment. His responsibilities as the oldest son demanded that he leave immediately, but there was another set of obligations that required him to do the opposite. "I knew every girl inside that building," he later told me. "These were my students—they were like sisters and daughters to me, and I could not leave them."

The streets were impassable, foreclosing any possibility of getting heavy equipment to the school, and the aftershocks were already triggering new spasms of vibration. Amid the dust and debris, the parents and the teachers could spy arms and legs and bits of clothing, so they went at the rubble with their bare hands. Muffled voices and screams helped guide the frantic rescuers to those who were still alive. Although the students who were pulled out were in shock, many of these survivors set to work separating the dead from injured, laying the corpses of their classmates out in the courtyard while caring for the stricken and the broken as best they could.

During that first morning and afternoon there was no drinking water, no medical supplies, and no blankets. At one point, Shaukat Ali helped remove the mangled body of a girl named Sabina, who had treated him like an older brother and had promised to help find him a wife. He could not bring himself to look at Sabina's face—and years later, he would still find it impossible to recall the moment he covered her body with a shawl without weeping. By evening, they had barely made a dent in the remains of the building.

The darkness that descended over the southwestern rim of the Vale of Kashmir that night was absolute, unbroken by a single lightbulb or streetlamp in the entire Neelum Valley. Then it started to rain.

This was not a soft patter or an intermittent drizzle, but a full-on deluge. The torrent rendered what was left of Patika cold and drenched. It fell so hard and so relentlessly that the ruins were swiftly filled with small rivers. They sluiced through the wreckage of the town's buildings, and they threaded around the bodies of its dead.

Shaukat Ali spent that night caring for a girl named Sura. Although she had been horribly injured and was in terrible pain, the only comfort he could offer was to hold her head in his lap and try to keep the rain from her face with his jacket. Long after midnight, when the rain had finally stopped, the aftershocks continued. He tried to keep track of the number, but stopped counting when he got to one hundred. The most haunting thing he remembered from that first night, however, he told me later, was the stillness between the convulsions.

Packs of *gidhad* (jackals) and wild dogs roam throughout the foothills of those mountains after sunset, and on any given night—especially during the *azan* (the muezzin's call to evening prayer), their howls tend to create a mournful racket that resounds across the ridgetops and through the valleys.

That night, not a single animal made a sound.

There is a twelve-hour time difference between Pakistan and the Rocky Mountains, and on the night of October 7, I was in a hotel room in Salt Lake City, where my son and daughter had a tae kwon do tournament scheduled for the following morning. When my wife, Tara, called shortly after 9:30 P.M. with news of the first damage reports from Kashmir, the kids and I had just returned from dinner at T.G.I. Friday's. Tara had no details, and I couldn't raise anyone in Pakistan. I tried to call Suleman, Saidullah, Parvi, Nazir, and every other person I could think of but couldn't get through—not even to Sarfraz on his satellite phone.

I asked Tara to keep trying to reach Suleman and if she got through, to tell him to keep in touch whenever and however possible. The kids wanted to go swimming, but before they did I sat them down on a bed and told them what had happened.

"Dad, how can we do a tae kwon do tournament tomorrow," asked Amira, "when the kids in Pakistan are dying?"

"Are Apo and Suleman okay?" chimed in Khyber, before telling me that I should immediately head off to Pakistan to help.

"It's hard to understand why there has to be suffering and tragedy like this in the world—and it's going to get worse," I told them as they clung tightly to my hands. "But we will do everything we can to help our friends over there. For now, let's say a prayer to keep them in God's hands."

Later that night, I jumped online. Tremors had been felt throughout central and southern Asia, and most of the early reports seemed to focus on the two apartment towers in Islamabad that had fallen down. As for the villages deep in the mountains and the people who lived near the quake's epicenter, I knew that it would be another several hours before details even started to emerge.

For now, my immediate concern was for the welfare of our staff and their families, followed closely by that of our teachers, students, and schools. The CAI projects that were closest to the epicenter were our pair of artillery-deflecting schools in Gultori, some eighty miles away. Many others were a hundred miles distant, certainly within range of a major quake.

By working the phones through most of that night and a good portion of the following day, I was able to confirm that all members of our operation and their families were safe and that all of our schools in Pakistan were still standing. There had been no deaths, not even any injuries, and only a minor crack in the lower wall of the Al Abid Primary School in Skardu. By that time, however, it had also become clear that the damage inside Kashmir was catastrophic.

Reports indicated that numerous towns and villages throughout northern Pakistan were completely wiped out. On each street and in every neighborhood, there were extended families in which every member of the clan—dozens of men, women, and children—had been killed instantly and interred together beneath the rubble of their homes. In the capital city of Muzaffarabad, the main hospital was demolished, killing more than two hundred patients. The city's prison had also pancaked, burying fifteen prisoners and wounding forty others while sixty survivors ran to safety. (One of the only structures left standing was a special set of gallows in the courtyard that could accommodate three condemned criminals at the same time.) Somewhere amid the wreckage of Muzaffarabad University, hundreds of college students had been buried alive. Families wandered the streets, refusing to return to their homes. Children, women, and men sat or stood in the open and wailed. By nightfall, dogs roamed the streets, tearing at the bodies of the dead until patrolling soldiers shot them down.

During the previous half century, Pakistan had suffered through four wars, two military coups, and any number of floods, bombings, political assassinations, and other disruptions, but there had never been anything quite like this. The trembler registered a magnitude of 7.6, approximately the same as the 1906 San Francisco earthquake. Satellite photos would later reveal that the quake had triggered 2,252 landslides, according to two American seismologists. Within a ten-mile radius of the town of Patika, there wasn't a single hospital bed, working telephone, or drop of municipal drinking water. The death toll according to the U.S. Geological Survey would eventually exceed eighty-six thousand, qualifying it as the worst natural disaster in the history of Pakistan, and the twelfth most destructive earthquake of all time.

A quarter of those casualties—nearly eighteen thousand dead—were children, most of them students who were in school when the earthquake struck. Strangely, the vast majority of those dead schoolchildren were girls, and as the debris was cleared away and the bodies were recovered, the explanation for this imbalance slowly emerged. While the boys had tended to race to safety by bolting out the windows and doors, most of the girls had instinctively huddled together and perished. Also, thanks to the government's tendency to channel the best resources toward male students before seeing to the needs of the females, many of the girls did not have desks—which might have saved thousands of lives had the girls been able to crawl under them for safety.

According to Pakistan's Ministry of Education, 3,794 schools and colleges in Kashmir and 2,159 in the Northwest Frontier Province had been destroyed. Roughly half a million students had been cut off from their studies. The education infrastructure for the region—offices, records, payrolls, everything—was gone, and more than five hundred teachers were dead. In less than four minutes, an entire generation of literate children had been wiped out.

It would take months before the extent of the destruction had been fully cataloged and analyzed. For the moment, the only thing the people of northern Pakistan really had was a name for what had befallen them.

In Urdu, the word for earthquake is *zalzala*. But throughout Kashmir, then and to this day, the event that took place on the morning of October 8 was simply known as the *Qayamat*—"the apocalypse."

Shaukat Ali spent all of Sunday, October 9, clawing at the rubble in search of injured girls, three of whom were pulled out alive. By now his hands were torn and his clothing was covered in blood. That night, the cries of girls who were trapped inside, which had been growing fainter, finally died out, leaving only silence. Just before noon on Monday, however, Shaukat Ali heard whimpers coming from the section of the wreckage where the fourth-grade classroom had been located. He and a group of men clawed feverishly at a hole in the rubble, dislodging a rain of stones and dirt.

"You idiot bastards, stop throwing rocks at us!" came a voice from within. "Can't you see that we are helpless and stuck?"

"This is your master Shaukat Ali," shouted Chaudry. "Are you okay?"

"We need water," came the response, "and we don't like you throwing stones at us when we have done nothing wrong!".

An hour later, a dozen men had cleared away several stones weighing more than two hundred pounds and a maze of twisted rebar to expose a pair of fourth graders named Aanam and Anii. They were surrounded by a close circle of fifteen of their dead friends, whose bodies had protected them from falling debris and cushioned the worst of the impact. Although Aanam and Anii could not see each other in the darkness and the dust, they had been holding hands for seventy-five hours.

After the girls were safely extracted, each guzzled a bottle of mineral water, then ran straight home. Later that evening, Shaukat Ali decided it was finally time for him to do the same.

When he reached the village of Batangi, he found his mother, Sahera Begum, huddled shivering in the rain under a sheet of plastic next to the ruins of their house. Nothing was left, not even her shoes or the family Koran. From his mother he learned that one of his sisters had been killed and already buried, along with his brother-in-law and all of his closest childhood friends. Of the 165 houses in his community, only 2 had been partially spared.

The following day, Shaukat Ali walked back into the center of Patika to purchase a shovel, a pick, some kerosene, and a pair of shoes for his mother. Then he returned home and started to dig out her belongings. With the help of his brothers and sisters, he spent that day and the next excavating the remains of her household and rigging a temporary shelter. Then on the seventh day, he walked twelve miles into the city of Muzaffarabad and was amazed by what he found.

Amid the wreckage and the chaos was a completely new town: a chaotic bazaar filled with supplies flown in from the world outside, new neighborhoods fashioned from tents and plastic, and most striking of all, new faces. The Red Cross, the Pakistani army, and the American army were all there, along with a host of international relief organizations, and the media. They were handing out free clothing and food, which Shaukat Ali could not bring himself to accept. He also refused to accept a job: The Red Cross desperately needed to hire translators, and people with his skills were in high demand. They were offering one hundred dollars a day in pay, more than he could make in a month. Instead, he went back to Patika and met with Saida Shabir, the principal of the Gundi Piran Girls' School.

A diminutive figure with dark eyes, thick glasses, and a limp, Shabir was nevertheless a formidable woman. She had been an educator for nearly thirty years, rising from teacher to administrator on the basis of a ferocious work ethic, and when she opened her mouth to express her displeasure, even the men stopped talking. She was known—and feared—for her fierce temper, her ability to make things happen fast, and a willingness to dress down any student, teacher, or government official who failed to conform to the standards she had set.

Shabir and Shaukat Ali agreed that although rebuilding the region's educational infrastructure hardly qualified as a top priority in the minds of the military and government officials who were spearheading the relief efforts, schools—especially girls' schools—were a potent symbol of progress. Getting classes up and running as quickly as possible could offer a beacon of hope for the entire community.

"Shaukat," ordered the headmistress, "go back down to Muzaffarabad, speak to the army commander who is in charge, and find out what sort of assistance he can offer."

Upon returning to Muzaffarabad, he approached a Pakistani army colonel who had been tasked with distributing relief supplies and explained that he needed several canvas tents so that he and Shabir could reopen their girls' school and resume classes. When the colonel realized that Shaukat Ali was serious, he called him a fool.

"Yes, that may be the case," replied Shaukat Ali. "But if the Pakistani army refuses to provide shelter, then we will have to begin teaching in the open air—and as you know, winter is just around the corner."

When he left Muzaffarabad, he had four eight-by-twelve-foot canvas tents—enough to accommodate six hundred students.

Back in Patika, he and Shabir agreed that time was short. All across Pakistan, government-administered schools would conduct final exams the following March, and if the girls of the Gundi Piran school were to have any chance of passing those tests, classes needed to resume as quickly as possible. Word was sent out that the school would reopen on November 1.

That afternoon, October 13, the rain finally stopped and it started to snow.

———

In the meantime, having returned home to Bozeman, I was anxious to survey the damage and talk with people on the ground. I realized, however, that it was probably more important for me to stay in the States for now. Our supporters and donors, old and new alike, would be sending in checks and wanting to know how we were going to spend the money. The mountaineering and the outdoor communities would surely want to donate tents, sleeping bags, parkas—and many of these people would be looking to us for guidance on how to get those supplies to Pakistan. All of which put me in a rather awkward and uncomfortable position.

Providing aid in the midst of a natural disaster is an extraordinarily complex and expensive job that presents almost impossible difficulties, even for organizations that specialize in this kind of work. The infrastructure for delivering food, providing shelter, and ensuring sanitation—not only for the victims but also for the relief workers—often has to be created from scratch and set up on the fly. Restoring power, transportation, communication, and proper medical care requires professionals with enormous expertise. In the face of such challenges, the notion that a group as tiny as the Central Asia Institute—an NGO that by then had built fewer than fifty schools on a budget of less than a million dollars a year—might somehow reinvent itself overnight as an emergency relief provider was well meaning but supremely impractical. We were not set up for emergency work, we knew almost nothing about the business of disaster relief, and with our new initiative in Afghanistan, our limited manpower and financial resources had already been stretched to the breaking point.

On the other hand, given what had just happened, a large chunk of northeastern Pakistan had just been cut off from the rest of the world and left to fend for itself. Whether we liked it or not, the residents of this region were now, quite literally, the people at the end of the road.

On October 10, Sarfraz finally called. He was already in the earthquake zone.

Sarfraz had felt the vibrations at his home in Zuudkhan, instantly grasped the significance of what had taken place, and hit the road. It had taken more than forty-eight hours for him to make his way to Islamabad and then head east, hitching rides in trucks, minivans, and jeeps and hiking over the sections that had been buried by landslides.

As soon as I heard his voice, I started grilling him about what was happening, but he told me to hold off with the questions. It would be several days, he explained, before he would be able to reach the most remote sections of the disaster area. Once there, he would take stock of the situation and report his findings back to me. Then we could decide together how the Central Asia Institute might be able to help. If we had a role to play, he suggested, it would depend heavily on what had happened to the local schools. For the moment, what we needed most was information.

His first destination was Balakot, a town on the eastern edge of Pakistan's Northwest Frontier Province. The scene that greeted him there was shocking. In some places, the road was lined with bodies waiting for relatives or friends to identify them for burial. In other places burials were already taking place, but thanks to a shortage of picks and shovels, people were digging graves with wooden boards or their bare hands. In one particular spot, he came upon a woman sitting by the debris from a collapsed school that her two daughters had attended. The rubble had already been pushed aside with a bulldozer, and the area had been combed by cadaver-sniffing dogs, who had failed to turn up any sign of her daughters, but the grieving mother refused to believe that her children's bodies were not inside. Sarfraz tried to console her, but she was refusing to eat, drink, or sleep.

From Balakot he continued working his way north up the Kaghan Valley, which is heavily populated by ethnic Pathans, a notoriously insular community. Many of these people seemed to react negatively to the idea that intruders from the outside were there to help. "Why are you coming here?" several locals demanded of Sarfraz. "We have no food or shelter for even our-selves—go away!"

Eventually Sarfraz managed to befriend an elderly Pathan named Mohammed Raza, who advised him that it would prob-ably be best if he left the area for now. The residents would even-tually begin turning their attention to the business of rebuilding schools, counseled Raza, but now was not the proper time. Should Sarfraz return in a year or two, he would probably meet with a better reception.

Based on the response he had received in the Kaghan, Sar-fraz's conclusion was pessimistic. If people didn't exactly wel-come *him,* a fellow Pakistani, how would they respond to the arrival of an American working for a foreign NGO like the Cen-tral Asia Institute? After returning to Islamabad and sharing his negative prognosis with me, he posed a difficult question.

If the Kaghan Valley would not work out, was it appropriate for us to start exploring the more remote areas that lay directly along the border between India and Pakistan—the places where outsiders had not ventured in years? In other words, should we consider venturing into the heart of Pakistan-administered Kashmir?

This made both of us pause to take a deep breath.

In addition to its notorious geological instability, Kashmir lies atop a web of political fault lines whose intractable complexity is matched only by the clash between the Israelis and the Palestinians. The origin of this conflict can be precisely dated to midnight on August 15, 1947, when Britain's Indian empire was officially partitioned into the new nations of India and Pakistan.

The upheaval of Partition produced one of the largest migrations of refugees in modern history (twenty-five million people) and the slaughter of nearly one million civilians, as Hindus and Sikhs fled south into India while Muslims raced in the opposite direction toward Pakistan. Another casualty was India's northernmost principality, the state of Jammu and Kashmir, which had a Muslim-majority population ruled by a Hindu maharaja named Hari Singh, whose great-grandfather had purchased Kashmir from the British in 1846 for 7.5 million rupees, or about 5 rupees per citizen—the cost of a cup of tea at an Indian roadside café.

Two months after Partition, Pakistan invaded Kashmir and rattled the composure of Hari Singh, a man whose interests up to that point had focused mostly on polo, late-night champagne parties, and shooting safaris. In the early hours of October 26, the maharaja fled the kingdom with his most exquisite jewels, his Webley & Scott shotguns, and his dog Tarzan. Meanwhile, the Indian government mobilized its entire fleet of passenger planes and airlifted three hundred Sikh troops into the capital city of Srinagar.

When the first round of fighting ended, two-thirds of Kashmir was in Indian hands, including Jammu, the Buddhist region of Ladakh, and the biggest prize of all, the legendary Vale of Kashmir. Pakistan controlled the regions of Gilgit and Baltistan, plus a sliver of southwestern Kashmir that India now refers to as Pakistan-Occupied Kashmir (POK) and Pakistan calls Azad Kashmir (Free Kashmir). On the map, Azad Kashmir is a narrow tongue of land, at some points only fifteen miles across, whose shape is similar to that of the Wakhan Corridor, but with a north-south orientation. The demarcation between the two

Kashmirs corresponds almost exactly to the final position of the battle lines when the military ceasefire was declared in January 1949. This 450-mile border, which starts near the Indian city of Jammu and cuts a diagonal, northeastward swath toward China, is known as the Line of Control (LOC).

In 1965 and again in 1971, India and Pakistan fought wars in Kashmir, both of which Pakistan lost. Then during the summer of 1989, a civil uprising exploded among ordinary Kashmiris who wanted independence from both India *and* Pakistan. Within months, the revolt had turned into a violent war that would eventually pit some sixty separate Islamic guerrilla groups against half a million Indian army troops and result in the deaths of more than thirty-six thousand people. Atrocities were committed on both sides. While Indian security forces detained, tortured, and executed civilians, Islamic militants who had been trained in Pakistan slipped across the border to attack Indian soldiers and carry out an assassination campaign against Hindu poets, judges, and social workers. The situation was not helped by the fact that twelve months earlier, Pakistan had conducted its first successful nuclear-weapons test.

Repression and reprisal followed one another until April 1999, when eight hundred Pakistan-supported militants launched a surprise attack across the Line of Control, seized a seventeen-thousand-foot ridge overlooking the cities of Kargil and Dras in India-controlled Kashmir, and began shelling a vital Indian military road that connects the cities of Srinagar and Leh. India responded with full force, and by early May there was heavy fighting along one hundred miles of the border. By July 4, when the Indian counterattack and pressure from the Clinton administration had forced Pakistani prime minister Nawaz Sharif to back down, both sides had reportedly put their nuclear strike forces on alert, provoking President Clinton to declare Kashmir "the most dangerous place on earth."

According to the United Nations, the final disposition of this disputed region—which has been pending for more than sixty years—is to be determined by a plebiscite among Kashmiri citizens, the majority of whom are still Muslim. Until that vote takes place and residents on both sides of the LOC are afforded the chance to exercise their UN-sanctioned right of self-determination, Kashmir is likely to remain inherently unstable and highly volatile.

By the time of the 2005 earthquake, Azad Kashmir had been closed to almost all foreigners for decades. As a result, despite having spent more than a dozen years living and working throughout Pakistan, I knew almost nothing about this place. The Central Asia Institute had no relationships, no connections, and no history in this part of the country. In short, we hadn't shared a single cup of tea in Azad Kashmir.

Given the magnitude of the disaster, however, the restrictions on foreign travel had been lifted overnight and NGOs from all over the world were now pouring into the area. So I suggested to Sarfraz that he should get back on the road and do his best to make his way into the eastern side of the damage zone, deep inside Azad Kashmir.

At this point, of course, neither Sarfraz nor I had ever heard of the Gundi Piran Girls' School—nor had we met Shaukat Ali Chaudry or Saida Shabir. But the events that would eventually draw all of us together had now been set in motion.

CHAPTER 8

No Idea What to Do

When your heart speaks, take good notes.
—Susan Campbell

Distribution point after earthquake, Neelum Valley, Pakistan

On October 15, Sarfraz again headed out of Islamabad, this time in the direction of Muzaffarabad, gateway to ground zero of the earthquake. The road he took proceeded east from Pakistan's capital and wound into the foothills past the idyllic summer resort of Murree, a former British hill station where lowlanders flee the Punjab's sweltering, humid heat in summer. From Murree, the road plunged down through a series of stunning canyons to the Kohala Bridge, which marks the entrance to the green hills of Azad Kashmir. Sarfraz was amazed to note that the Frontier Works Organization (FWO), Pakistan's military civil-engineering unit, had already managed to clear more than a dozen massive landslides and open the road. But upon rounding the bend into Muzaffarabad, which sits at the confluence of the Neelum and Jhelum rivers, he found himself confronted once again with the sort of carnage and suffering he had already witnessed in the Kaghan Valley.

Almost every structure in the city was cracked, leaning, or collapsed. Each street and alley was crowded with homeless, wandering, injured, or traumatized adults and children whose emotional stability was not helped by the numerous aftershocks. In every neighborhood, Pakistani army crews were sifting through wreckage searching for bodies and any possible survivors. People were milling everywhere, dazed and looking for food and water.

Sarfraz spent that first night in a sleeping bag on the sidewalk outside the Al-Abbas Hotel and Restaurant, which was perched on a cliff high above the Neelum River (and which the members of the Dirty Dozen would eventually dub the Crack Hotel on account of the massive vertical fissure that zigzagged down one side of the structure). The next day, as he moved about the city, he called me on his sat phone to report that there would be an inevitable bias toward concentrating most emergency supplies in Muzaffarabad in order to use the city as the staging area for the whole region. This, Sarfraz went on to explain, was good news to the residents of Muzaffarabad; but it would offer little comfort to the 2.5 million displaced people in the surrounding valleys and hillsides who were cut off from most contact with the outside world.

After laying this out, Sarfraz proposed that he head northeast in an effort to reach the most remote villages along the most distant reaches of the Neelum Valley, a 150-mile-long gorge carved by the Neelum River, which is named after the color of the rubies that can be mined at various points along its folds, and which once served as one of the world's most important centers of Buddhism. Thanks to its precipitous canyon walls and the fact that it had received some of the heaviest Indian artillery shelling during the past two decades, the Neelum qualified as perhaps the most underserved district in all of Azad Kashmir. By virtue of these attributes, argued Sarfraz, this was probably where we would want to target our work. (Although we didn't know this at the time, more than 10 percent of the valley's 140,000 residents had perished in the earthquake, and the majority of these victims were schoolchildren.)

I told him I agreed completely, and I wished him luck.

Sarfraz had hired a car to bring him this far, but when he saw the condition of the road beyond Muzaffarabad, he sent the driver back to Islamabad and continued on foot, carrying several bottles of water, his sleeping bag, and a package of salted crackers. The road up the Neelum Valley was blocked by dozens of landslides, and in some areas entire slabs of mountain had crashed into the river.

As he threaded his way through the mud and the debris, everyone whom he spoke to had a story, and every story was tragic. Without exception, each person he encountered had lost at least one close relative, usually more. Anyone who had been inside a building was lucky to be alive, although most of them had lost all of their worldly possessions. It seemed like nearly everyone was limping or had a field dressing that was matted with dried blood. Men and women either carried two or three children on their backs or pushed their families along in a wheelbarrow. With his sleeping bag and his package of biscuits, Sarfraz qualified as a man of enviable riches.

That night, while sleeping under a smashed truck, he called me on his sat phone. "The roads are filled with people: people walking, people looking for food, people crying," he reported. "It is very bad everywhere. When it is dark and when nobody is looking, even I start to cry."

Most natural disasters are followed by a high degree of chaos, and the first goal of the authorities is to try systematically to reduce that chaos. But in Azad Kashmir during the second week of October, things only seemed to become more confused and more disorganized with each passing day. Within forty-eight hours, the only two roads leading from Islamabad into the devastated valleys to the north were jammed with every kind of conveyance, including donkey, bicycles, and rickshaws, as relatives and friends poured into the province in the hope of finding loved ones. From all across Pakistan, well-intentioned volunteers were now rushing into the mountains to offer assistance. As a result, the few stretches of highway that had not already been blocked by landslides were now hopelessly gridlocked. At one point, the Pakistani army began bulldozing vehicles off the road in order to get the flow of traffic going.

Adding to the confusion was the flurry of international assistance that was converging on the stricken region. The international NGOs needed a plethora of ancillary support, including Land Cruisers, kitchens, generators, remote servers for their laptops, mineral water, and much more. In order to facilitate the flow of humanitarian and medical aid, five crossing points along the LOC between India and Pakistan had been opened—but these thoroughfares were soon bottlenecked as aid teams began arriving from around the world. Twelve days after the quake, the Pakistani government still had not reached 20 percent of the damaged areas. Two weeks after that, the U.N. World Food Program would estimate that five hundred thousand people still had not received any aid at all. By the middle of November, more than three million refugees would be huddling in the mountains without shelter or adequate food on the threshold of the winter.

As Sarfraz headed north, hiking first from Muzaffarabad to Patika and then proceeding for seventeen hours from Patika to the village of Nousada, he could see that in many places the landslides that had destroyed the roads had also obliterated entire communities. Ten miles north of Muzaffarabad, for example, lay the Kamsar refugee camp, home to about a thousand Muslim refugees from India-controlled Kashmir who had been living there since 1992. The camp had been situated on a narrow bench approximately two thousand feet above the Neelum River; during the quake, half of the settlement had broken off the hillside and plunged into the gorge, taking with it more than three hundred of the camp's residents. The buildings on the portion of the bench that remained intact had all been destroyed, rendering the seven hundred survivors refugees twice over.

Three days after leaving Muzaffarabad, Sarfraz reached the village of Nouseri, where every house had been obliterated and people were wandering the trail in rags, still unable to fathom what had taken place and having not the faintest notion of where or how to begin rebuilding their lives. Eight miles farther on, in the tiny hamlet of Pakrat, he met a woman named Alima whose husband and two children had perished in the quake. She was squatting atop a wooden bed outside the remains of her home, staring blankly at a sheaf of papers. These were the official documents that she was supposed to fill out in order to qualify for a government disbursement of cash. In addition to being immobilized by her despondency, Alima was illiterate.

"I asked the *fauji havildar* (army sargeant) for help," she said to Sarfraz, "and all he gave me was this piece of paper—and when I started to complain and ask for food, he told me to go away or he would beat me with his stick. This paper is not even food enough for a dog."

Alima's predicament struck Sarfraz as twisted and surreal, a kind of satire of cruelty. The forms that she was supposed to fill out featured a slew of questions to which she had no answer, including the place and date of her birth, her age, and her national identification number.

"How is a woman like this ever going to survive?" he exclaimed that night on the sat phone. "Everywhere I am looking, there are dead bodies, and the people who are not dead act like they are dead. This is too much. No one has any idea of what to do."

Sarfraz is a resilient man who has lived a challenging life, but the scenes he was encountering in Azad Kashmir were beginning to grind him down. Each night, his report to me was depressingly the same. In every direction, from every angle, the world seemed to be filled with chaos and despair.

One of the few bright spots to which Sarfraz could point during his reconnaissance trips involved Operation Lifeline, an internationally organized effort to transport emergency supplies via helicopter into isolated villages and towns all across Azad Kashmir. This mission included several choppers provided by the British and the Germans, along with a number of Pakistan's own Soviet-era Mi-17 helicopters. The heart and soul of the operation, however, involved fourteen American Chinooks flown by an Army Reserve unit from Olathe, Kansas. These machines, along with their two hundred pilots and support crew, were the unsung heroes of the early relief effort.

The Chinooks had flown in straight from the war in Afghanistan within two days of the quake, and their first mission involved ferrying bulldozers, trucks, and other heavy equipment necessary to rebuild the main roads, while using their return flights to evacuate the severely injured. Later, they hauled tents, roofing materials, medical supplies, flour, cement, baby formula, and anything else that might be needed—including a special consignment of sewing machines. The 6,000 tons of material that the helicopters delivered in the first three months following the earthquake—one of the most massive helicopter airlifts ever conducted—was eventually credited with keeping half a million people alive over the ensuing winter.

As the choppers penetrated ever deeper into the damage zone, their fame increased, and eventually the toys that were most coveted by the children of Azad Kashmir were little plastic helicopters. Everyone loved the Chinooks and their crews, who were invariably greeted with waves and cheers and, of course, hordes of kids. Sarfraz talked to some of the pilots and learned that those who had served in Iraq could not believe that the people of Pakistan actually *liked* them. In the coming years, many of these pilots and their crew members would look back upon those weeks as the highlight of their military careers.

As the Chinooks delivered their payloads of heavy equipment and as the traffic jams were sorted out, the roads gradually began to open up. By the middle of October, Sarfraz reported that Muzaffarabad had become command central for the entire relief effort as the big international aid organizations—UNICEF, Oxfam, the Red Cross, CARE, the Red Crescent Society, and more than a dozen others—erected satellite dishes, set up computer banks, and began stockpiling supplies. But "upside" in the more remote communities, there was little evidence of this progress, which created a troubling dichotomy. In downtown Muzaffarabad, for example, Sarfraz saw six large emergency field hospitals lined up in a row, each equipped with generators and surgical supplies. A village only ten miles away, however, might have received absolutely nothing. Six months after the earthquake—in some instances even a year later—Sarfraz was still hearing about villages that had not received a single ounce of aid.

Another problem was lack of coordination. In the earliest weeks of the catastrophe, the supplies that were flown in by helicopter were distributed almost randomly. Whenever a helicopter began heading up a valley, everyone could hear it coming, and the race was on. The supplies were distributed on a first-come-first-served basis, and many of the scenes that unfolded on the chopper landing zones were quite unpleasant.

In some areas, a refugee camp stocked with tents, clothes, and food would simply materialize—courtesy of the Chinooks—and thousands of people would rush in to grab what they could. A week later, another camp might be set up four miles away, and everyone would rush *there*. Amid the "every man for himself" atmosphere, some people enjoyed a windfall while others wound up with nothing.

By the end of October, Sarfraz was also starting to notice an odd gap between what was being delivered and what people actually needed. A number of outdoor manufacturers from the United States, for example, had donated impressive quantities of high-tech mountaineering tents made with synthetic fabrics that are highly flammable. As the weather turned cold, these tents became crammed with families who relied on candles and kerosene lanterns for illumination and who prepared their meals on cooking fires directly outside the front flap. Many of these tents ended up catching fire, resulting in horrific burns and several deaths, especially among children. In retrospect, low-tech, heavy-duty canvas shelters would have been more effective and less dangerous.

A notable exception to this trend were the "home-rebuilding kits" donated by the Turkish government after significant consultation with refugees on the ground. The kits, which Turkish officials purchased in Pakistan, consisted of hammers, nails, shovels, saws, wire, corrugated sheet metal, and other essential building items so that people could fashion temporary shelters in their own villages instead of packing up and moving to a refugee camp. When I later asked people in Azad Kashmir what had benefited them the most during the aftermath of the earthquake, the reply was fairly consistent: getting the roads reopened and the Turkish home-construction kits.

By early November, Sarfraz was starting to see groups of women who would bundle up huge bales of donated clothing—

expensive waterproof parkas, pants, and bibs—and set them on fire to heat water or for cooking. It turned out that what these women really needed was an efficient source of cooking fuel, and without a steady supply of kerosene or propane, they were forced to prepare their families' meals over fires made from The North Face, Patagonia, and Mountain Hardwear gear.

This clothing was used for other purposes as well. Later that month, Sarfraz e-mailed me a photograph of a sheep grazing on a hillside with a puffy down jacket wrapped around its hind end. Clearly, what these refugees needed was building material with which to fabricate shelters to keep their livestock alive. Since no one had asked them, however, they were doing their best to improvise. The instinct to help was wonderful, but one can only imagine what the down jacket donor would have thought if he or she had seen what his or her gift eventually was used for. The sheep photo graphically illustrated the limitations of simply fire hosing relief supplies into an area without proper coordination.

Such chaotic methods sometimes provoked cynicism and exacerbated people's frustration. On one trip, Sarfraz met a police officer from Muzaffarabad named Qurban Ali Shah, whose father had been killed in the quake. This man was quick to pull out an impressive sheaf of calling cards collected from various individuals and aid groups who had arrived in the city over the preceding weeks. One was from a Chinese doctor, another from a German "emergency architect." Dozens of these people had passed their contact information along to Qurban Ali Shah, and not one of them had ever followed up. All he had to show was his collection of business cards.

In other instances, expressions of international concern that failed to result in concrete action provoked feelings of betrayal and anger. Such was the case at the Gundi Piran school, where the tragedy itself and the valiant rescue efforts became a focal point for the international broadcast media, whose representatives flew in on quick helicopter jaunts to obtain graphic visuals for their broadcasts. According to teachers at Gundi Piran, crews from major television networks based in Britain, France, the United States, Germany, Japan, and Italy all descended on the school, along with dozens of reporters from various radio stations, newspapers, and magazines. A number of these journalists apparently reacted angrily when headmistress Saida Shabir, in order to protect her staff and students' fragile emotional state, prevented the reporters from conducting intrusive interviews with them. Months later, Shabir regretted having given them any access to the school whatsoever. Despite the massive news coverage, she said, she had yet to receive a single substantive gesture of assistance—not one brick, not one pen—from an NGO or a member of the Pakistani government. No one had even helped to provide decent funerals or burials for the seven girls who had been pulled from the wreckage of the school and whose bodies had never been claimed—presumably because their entire families had been killed.

In the end, Shaukat Ali and several other members of the faculty were forced to dig a set of graves themselves and to lay the girls to rest in the courtyard of the ruined school.

Unfortunately, some of the smartest and most effective assistance was provided by groups of Islamic militants. Within seventy-two hours of the earthquake, Al Qaeda's number two leader, Ayman al-Zawahiri, issued a dramatic videotaped message urging Muslims around world to help the victims of this disaster. "I call on all Muslims in general, and I call on all Islamic humanitarian associations in particular, to move to Pakistan to provide help to their Pakistani brothers, and that they do it quickly," he declared. "All of us know the vicious American war on Muslim humanitarian work."

In response, resourceful and energetic young *jihadis* were often the first to show up during the earthquake's aftermath, in many cases appearing days or even weeks before the Pakistani army or the international aid organizations arrived. According to Ahmed Rashid, author of *Descent Into Chaos* and the foremost independent journalist reporting from Afghanistan and Pakistan, seventeen extremist groups that were either on the United Nations' list of terrorist organizations or banned by the Pakistani government were reactivated during this time as Islamic NGOs. They did an impressive job of putting together sophisticated relief operations, delivering supplies and medical care to victims with speed and efficiency when no one else could.

One of the first such groups on the scene was Jamaat-ud-Dawa, the political arm of the banned extremist militia Lashkar-e-Taiba, the pro-Taliban, Pakistan-based organization that would carry out the horrific terrorist attacks in Bombay in November 2008 that resulted in the deaths of 173 civilians. Another elaborate operation was run by the extremely conservative group Jamaat-e-Islami. After setting up base camps in several ravaged towns, Jamaat's Al-Khidmat Foundation began dispatching its operatives to remote areas where motorized vehicles could not penetrate. Not far from the Jamaat-e-Islami operation in Muzaffarabad was another camp sponsored by the Al Rashid Trust, which was created by Dr. Amir Aziz, a British-trained orthopedic surgeon who has admitted to treating Al Qaeda leaders, including Osama bin Laden.

Amid the rush to provide tents, food, and medical supplies, few of the western NGOs seemed to be giving much thought to schools. Based on past experience, however, the militant groups who were busy setting up their aid networks fully understood the power of education under such circumstances. Back in the winter of 1989, when the Soviets had pulled out of Afghanistan and the country was struggling to get back on its feet after ten years of war, the Saudi government had sponsored thousands of conservative madrassas, religious institutions open only to boys and designed to instill a fundamentalist interpretation of Islamic law. During the 1990s, about eighty thousand boys who had received hard-line religious instruction in these madrassas were fed directly into the ranks of the Taliban. Now, it seemed a similar dynamic was beginning to unfold in Azad Kashmir. Within a year, a number of these camps would become fertile recruiting grounds for Islamic militants looking for new followers.

Inside one refugee camp that I saw in Muzaffarabad, the mess tent where families came to receive their daily rations had been set up directly adjacent to an enormous tent that functioned as a madrassa where young boys were being tutored on the nuances of jihad. Many of the refugee parents were not happy about the fact that their children were attending these extremist schools, but because the *jihadis* were providing them with food, shelter, and medicine, they were reluctant to object.

Combining aid with ideology was a highly effective strategy—and this same formula would repeat itself four years later when two million Pakistani civilians were displaced by the Pakistani army's offensive against the Taliban in the Swat Valley. (By the summer of 2009, hard-line Islamist charities had established precisely the same kind of foothold and were pushing their anti-western agenda among the residents of the Swat refugee camps.)

I have always been dismayed by the West's failure—or unwillingness—to recognize that establishing secular schools that offer children a balanced and nonextremist form of education is probably the cheapest and most effective way of combating this kind of indoctrination. Despite the fact that the American government has never grasped its importance, this calculus has been at the heart of what we do from the very beginning—and with Sarfraz in the lead, we continued to pursue this agenda in Azad Kashmir during the winter of 2005.

By January, Sarfraz had managed to commandeer several UNICEF tents from army depots in Balakot and Muzaffarabad. After transporting these tents to the most distant villages in the Neelum Valley, such as Nouseri, Pakrat, and Behdi, Sarfraz set about identifying the leaders—the most energetic people, who were the survivors in the broad sense of the word. With their help, he then located teachers, arranged for their salaries, and then started rounding up the parents and kids in order to get the schools going.

Within a couple of months, Sarfraz had set up more than a dozen of these little operations in places that lay beyond the reach of the most outstretched NGO or government authority. Needless to say, in a region where every school in every community had been completely destroyed, this was barely a drop in the bucket. But everyone who works with the Central Asia Institute believes in the value and the power of this little drop. On the grand scale of things, Sarfraz's tent schools were miniscule; but among the people at the end of the road, these projects offered a catalyst for hope.

Amid the devastation of Kashmir that autumn, this is what passed for sharing three cups of tea.

Meanwhile, back in Montana, I was not having an easy time of things. Within hours of the earthquake, the e-mails, phone calls, letters, and checks were pouring into our little two-room office in Bozeman. The people who were calling and writing were often quite insistent about the fact that as far as they were concerned we had the resources and the connections to help in this disaster—and they expected us to do something immediately.

Truth be told, however, I had no idea what the CAI could or should do at this point—and indeed, the entire purpose of Sarfraz's reconnaissance trips was to collect the information that would enable us to make wise decisions and distribute our resources intelligently. That was my message to the people who were contacting us, but at the time my methodical and pragmatic approach didn't seem to carry much weight. Throughout October, donors flooded our office with tents, clothing, and outdoor gear; and attached to each contribution was a request, implicit or otherwise, that we please do something—*anything*—to assist the stricken citizens of Pakistan during their bleakest hour of need.

Many of our supporters also sent money, and by the week before Thanksgiving, we were sitting on more than $160,000 that needed to be spent in behalf of education.

As I huddled in my basement office listening to Sarfraz report on the confusion and the despair, the madrassas, and all the other things he was witnessing, the most powerful reaction I experienced was a deep sense of guilt over my absence from the front lines. At night, I would wake up at about 2:00 A.M. with the refugees on my mind and find myself unable to get back to sleep. Then at 4:30, I would drive over to Gold's Gym to work out with Jeff McMillan, a trainer who is also a friend and who frequently stops by to assist Tara and the kids during my long absences. Nothing seemed to help, however, and I quickly became trapped in an obsession with the fact that I simply wasn't doing enough. It was finally Tara, who understands me better than any other human being, who decided to act.

"Let's go out to dinner tonight," she said. "We need to talk."

When we got to the restaurant, she got straight to the point.

"Sweetie, if you just stay here you are going to drive yourself and the rest of us crazy. So when we get home, I'm going to pull out your duffel bags, and I want you to start packing. It's time for you to go and do what you do best. This is your calling. And when you get home, we will be here waiting for you."

The timing was terrible—the holidays were just around the corner, and as Tara and I both knew, if I left now there was no way I could be back home for Christmas. This was a very difficult decision, and in the end, the person who made it on my behalf was my wife and best friend. She knew that although I was home, I was not really home—and in order to return home with full heart and mind, I needed to leave now.

On Thanksgiving morning, I was on my way.

CHAPTER 9

Farzana's Desks

But once the ruins fluttered with voices and we
came upon an improvised school. . . . In the sunlight falling
through the fractured walls, the children turned
to stare at us, clear-faced and smiling.
—COLIN THUBRON, *Shadow of the Silk Road*

House destroyed in earthquake, Azad Kashmir, Pakistan

Over the next six weeks, shifting combinations of Sarfraz, myself, and the Pakistani members of the Dirty Dozen penetrated into the furthest corners of the Neelum Valley. Occasionally we hitchhiked, once or twice we rode donkeys, but mostly we just walked. We subsisted on crackers and ramen noodles, we drank river water treated with iodine tablets, and we slept beneath wrecked vehicles on the road or under a tarp. When Sarfraz and I were alone, we moved even further into what we referred to as our lean-and-mean mode, dozing for three hours a night and keeping ourselves going by swallowing handfuls of ibuprofen and guzzling endless cups of tea. I called Tara every now and then, but the horror that surrounded us robbed me of the energy to think much about home.

I quickly discovered that Sarfraz had not exaggerated the extent of the destruction and the misery. Even now, nearly two months after the quake, thousands of people were still missing. Were they dead, injured, in a refugee camp, or staying with relatives somewhere else? No one knew, partly because the search crews were still uncovering bodies from the wreckage, and partly because everyone seemed to be on the move.

The roads were filled with little groups of men, almost always from the same community, who had ventured forth together in search of a distribution point where they could obtain food and shelter for their relatives and neighbors. Once they discovered a camp that was stocked with these supplies, these men would join up and then send word back to their home village for more people to come down. Soon enough, almost all of the survivors of a destroyed village would have relocated en masse. The camps in which they congregated reminded me of the Afghan refugee settlements I had often visited on the opposite side of Pakistan— overwhelmed by the stench of human waste and lacking sanitation, sewage treatment, and adequate drinking water. At night, people struggled to sleep in close-packed tents. During the day, they milled around with nothing to do.

Over time, some of these camps broke up as the supplies evaporated, forcing the residents to disperse and move on. In other cases, the camp might emerge as a semipermanent supply hub and begin transforming into something that resembled an actual community. Under such circumstances, the refugees would begin finding menial jobs and replacing their plastic-tarp shelters with shacks cobbled together from construction scraps.

This changing human dynamic drew us into the refugee camps, too. Once inside, we'd ask what village the people were from, how many children were in their community, and whether their schools had survived the quake. The answer to this last question, we discovered, was always no. In the fifty or sixty villages of the upper Neelum Valley, every single school had been completely destroyed. We thought there might be an exception somewhere, but if there was, we never found it.

Each of the schools in this region had hosted anywhere from 150 to 600 students, and in almost every case, between a third and half of the children had perished. Shoddy construction was often the main culprit. In many instances, the government sub-contractors who had put up these buildings had cut corners by placing their roof beams forty or more inches apart (the spacing should be no more than twenty-eight inches). Others had also used a sand-to-cement ratio of ten to one (as opposed to six to one) or had failed to employ rebar or double-cast steel for reinforcement.

The resulting structural failures tended to conform to one of two patterns: Either the roof had come apart and the pieces had fallen directly onto the children's heads, or the walls had disintegrated and the roof had crashed down as a solid unit. In the latter situation, it was not unusual for every single student to have died. In the tiny village of Nousada, 198 students were buried alive in this manner. Three years later, in the summer of 2009, the cement roof slab was still splayed across the side of the hill where the school had once stood. To this day, it continues to serve as a memorial stone marking the mass grave of the children of Nousada.

Within these remote villages, there was often very little government or NGO activity for the purpose of providing food or medical care and no effort whatsoever to address education needs. In a few places, the Pakistani army had erected a large tent and announced that it was now the local school, but this was rarely adequate. In such traumatized communities, it was necessary to find someone who was capable of teaching—or to bring in a teacher from the surrounding area—and then to support that person with books, teaching materials, and a salary. In the area where we were focusing most of our efforts, Sarfraz's tent schools were often the only institutions that seemed to have any staying power.

Throughout December and the first part of January, we paid visits to each of the communities where Sarfraz had started a tent school in order to find out what kind of support was needed to keep them going. In the communities Sarfraz had not yet visited, we started this process from scratch. The initial results were often chaotic and confusing.

The key was to find one or two dedicated teachers around whom we could establish the school. If we had over one hundred students per teacher, we set up two shifts of three or four hours each, one shift for the boys, another shift for the girls, with the older students helping the younger ones. Given the extent to which people were moving around, a certain school might have two hundred students one day and four hundred students the next. The teachers came and went with equal unpredictability as they tried to put their lives back together.

Obviously, this was less than ideal, but often it was the best we—or anyone—could do. Given our limited manpower and resources in these mountains, our follow-up work during the first months after the catastrophe wasn't as tight as it needed to be. Nevertheless, during the winter of 2005–6, someone from our local staff visited each of these tent schools every week or two in order to pay the teachers, monitor the progress of the students, and make arrangements for supplies to be delivered. In the absence of assistance from the government or the big international aid organizations, this was the only help that these communities would get for now—and often the impact was significant. Despite the fact that classes were supposed to be in recess during the coldest months of winter, heroic teachers labored to keep the schools running so that their students would not get behind. This became a point of pride in many of the devastated communities. Parents would bring tea and chapattis for the students' lunch, then sit in the back of the class, listening to the lessons and ready to step in and help if asked.

During this time, the manner in which people responded to us changed, too. Slowly but surely, word began to spread about the odd couple of Azad Kashmir: the broken-handed Ismaili from the Charpurson Valley and his lumbering, bear-shaped American sidekick dressed in a mud-colored *shalwar kamiz*. And gradually, relationships began to take root.

Sarfraz and I never presented ourselves as emergency-relief workers, but people knew that we wanted to help. This counted for a lot, especially in places where no one else from the outside world, except for the Chinook crews, had managed to pay a visit. But what counted even more, I think, was the fact that in each community we made a point of consulting with the elders and the parents in order to find out what *they* thought they needed. In a way, even though we had come into this stricken valley in order to build schools and to promote education, we were inviting the people of the area to become *our* teachers. And in so doing, Sarfraz and I wound up relearning the lesson that had originally been imparted to me, all those years ago, by the silver-bearded Haji Ali in the village of Korphe.

When you take the time to actually listen, with humility, to what people have to say, it's amazing what you can learn. Especially if the people who are doing the talking also happen to be children.

Farzana was a beautiful ninth grader with deep brown eyes and dense black eyebrows who lived in the village of Nouseri. Her story bore the same dimensions of tragedy and loss that had marked the lives of all the surviving children of Nouseri, where more than a third of the community's 1,500-odd residents had been killed and only a handful of homes were still standing.

Farzana's mother, Jamila Khattoon, and her twelve year-old brother, Nabil, had been killed inside their house when the roof collapsed. Two miles down the road lay the ruins of the local girls' school where Farzana's thirteen-year-old sister, Sidra, was one of forty-seven students killed. Aside from Farzana herself, the surviving members of her family included her father, Nur Hussein, a veteran of the Pakistani army, and her three-year-old sister, Kurat.

The weeks following the earthquake left little time for grieving. Nouseri's water system had been completely destroyed, which meant that every day, Farzana and the other women of the village were obliged to hike two miles and descend three thousand feet to the river and climb back up carrying fifty-pound jugs filled with water. Meanwhile, Nur Hussein had to leave the village each morning for a six-hour round-trip hike to the nearest Pakistani army camp, where he collected the family's daily allotment of flour, plus some cooking oil, salt, and tea.

When Sarfraz and I made it to Nouseri, the surviving students were supposed to be studying their lessons in one of the tent schools that Sarfraz had set up on an earlier visit. Attendance at this school, however, was extremely spotty. The kids were around—we could see them moving about the village—but most of them were avoiding the school and did not even seem to want to come near it. No one could tell us why, until one day when I was sitting on the floor of the tent school with the teacher and the handful of kids who were willing to attend class, including Farzana.

Before I left Bozeman, my wife, who is a psychotherapist and often works with traumatized women, had advised me to encourage the children who had survived the earthquake to talk, draw, write, or even sing about their experience—anything that might enable them to get their feelings out in the open would start the healing process, she said. So during a lull in the class, I cleared my throat and posed a question.

"Would anyone like to talk about the earthquake today?"

There was dead silence. Several of the children glared. One of the girls ran out of the tent, sat down by the door, and started to cry, wiping her eyes with her *dupatta* (head scarf).

Well, now you've really gone and done it, Greg, I thought to myself.

Then a quiet, low voice came from the back corner of the tent. It was Farzana, whose little sister, Kurat, was clinging to her back.

"Let me tell you for all of us," she began.

There was a long pause and some reshuffling. The girl who had been sitting outside in tears padded softly back into the tent.

"*Bismillah ir-Rahman Rakham ir-Rahim,*" Farzana spoke. "In the name of Allah, the Merciful, the Beneficent."

"This is very difficult for all of us," she continued. "The day of the Qayamat is like a black night that we want to forget, so please forgive us for being so sad."

In painstaking detail, she went on to describe the quake itself—pausing often to keep herself from breaking down, allowing time for her fellow students to insert a murmured comment.

"We were just starting school when a strange roar came up the valley, like a lion, and then there was a quiet few seconds, which was followed by a violent ruffling, like an old man shaking the base of a young apricot tree as hard as he could. Then after a minute, it was quiet again. And then there was a ripple in the whole mountain—like a wave on the water."

Everyone nodded.

At that point, explained Farzana, the buildings started to collapse. The walls disintegrated first, then the roofs came down in an explosive shower of concrete and wood. As the buildings shattered, clouds of dust rose from the debris and the sky turned dark. Then the screaming began, and over the screams you could hear the shouts of the parents who were running down the hill from the village to find their children. Within minutes, the clatter of picks and shovels arose as the men started attacking the rubble. There were fewer screams now—it was mostly moans and crying. And the air was still thick with dust.

Farzana's description of the events of that morning was very vivid and exceptionally detailed, and something about not only the precision of her words but also the manner in which her thoughts and emotions seemed to play across her face as she spoke led me to wonder if she might be able to clear up the confusion surrounding the school's attendance problem.

When she was finished, I asked her why so few kids were coming to class.

"Because there are no desks in the tents," she said matter-of-factly.

This was interesting, but also odd. In this part of the world, many homes lack chairs and people are much more comfortable sitting on the floor. In many of our schools across Pakistan and Afghanistan, it is not unusual for an entire class to sit cross-legged on the floor while the teacher stands. The lack of desks seemed like a strange reason not to go to school.

"Why are desks so important?" I asked.

"They make children feel safe," she explained. "And with desks, the tents feel more like a real school."

This seemed to make sense, and I nodded, but she wasn't finished.

"But even if the classes are held outside, you should have desks outside, too," she said. "Only then will the children come to class."

This seemed rather mysterious, but something about Farzana's earnest directness made me want to trust her. So the next day Sarfraz and I began rummaging around a pile of rubble in the remains of the girls' school and scavenged the shattered remains of several dozen desks. That afternoon, we rounded up a few men and paid them to start refurbishing. Word of this activity spread quickly, and within an hour or two of our installing the desks in the tent, dozens of kids were filing into class.

What Farzana had understood was that in the minds of the

children, desks provided concrete evidence that at least within the confines of their classroom, a degree of order, stability, and normalcy had returned to their lives. In a traumatized world where everything had been turned upside down and the ground itself had given way, a desk offered certitude. It was something you could trust.

That marked the beginning of "Operation School Desk."

Armed with Farzana's insight, we started retrieving the remains of broken furniture from every possible source, and over the next week, our team of amateur carpenters knocked together about eight hundred desks for every tent school in the area. But it didn't end there. Other organizations in Balakot and Muzaffarabad got wind of Farzana's insight, and soon schools up and down the Neelum Valley were filling up with desks. From that time forward, desks became a requirement for all of the tent schools we established in Azad Kashmir.

In terms of solving the staggering crisis besetting Azad Kashmir, this desk business barely merited notice. It did, however, represent a small step forward during a moment when almost nothing seemed to be going well. And more important, perhaps, it was something that had been initiated by the children themselves.

As I was about to discover, however, it wasn't simply the children of Kashmir who had something to say to us.

In the middle of January, I was forced once again to say farewell to Sarfraz and return home to Montana. I was loath to leave the earthquake zone, but the run-up to the publication of *Three Cups of Tea* was in full swing, and this would offer a chance to raise some much-needed funds for our work in Pakistan and Afghanistan.

Back in Bozeman, as I struggled to immerse myself in the

endless rounds of phone calls and e-mails, all I could really think about were the survivors whom I'd left behind in Azad Kashmir. I found myself dwelling on the disparity between the urgent work that needed doing over there and what struck me as the rather mundane office tasks that I was performing in the United States. Within a week of getting home, I was depressed, disengaged, and already plotting how to return to Pakistan.

That's where things stood one evening in late January as I was reading a bedtime story to Khyber, who was five years old at the time. *He* was happy I was home, and that made me happy, too. Moreover, reading to him and Amira had always been one of Tara's and my favorite things to do. But as I read the words to *Where the Wild Things Are* by Maurice Sendak, tracing each sentence with my finger, my mind was preoccupied with issues on the opposite end of the planet.

What time was it in Kashmir, and where was Sarfraz right now, and when would he be calling? How many teachers were on our payroll in the Neelum Valley at the moment, and did I need to wire funds to Islamabad in order to cover their salaries for this month?

Oh my goodness!

My reverie was derailed by the realization that my son had stopped listening to my voice and begun to enunciate the words on the page for himself. He was not reciting these words from memory. Khyber was reading for the first time in his life.

When you are a parent, the instant your child first begins to read is a moment of the purest magic. It doesn't matter whether you happen to live in Kashmir or Montana or Tanzania or Manhattan—witnessing the fire of literacy ignite in the mind of a child is something transcendent. To me, it felt exactly like releasing the string on a helium-filled balloon and watching it ascend into the sky all by itself.

But there was another feeling, too. Mixed with the intoxicating sense of buoyancy was an awareness of the many other milestones in the lives of my children that I had irrevocably missed. Their first steps. Their first spoken words. Their first bike rides. Their first day of school.

These developments, which are the delight of so many parents, had all unfolded while I was at work on the far side of the world, attending to the needs and the dreams of other people's children. And yet right now, I was permitted to be lying next to my own son for this one precious moment. The piercing combination of joy and loss was too much to bear, and the tears began rolling down my face.

This was deeply puzzling to Khyber, who had no way of grasping the enormity of this moment for his father.

"Daddy, what's the matter? Are you okay?" he asked, comforting me with a pat on the shoulder.

"Yes, Khyber, I'm okay, and I'm so proud of you today," I responded. "You know how to read!"

Khyber then called out to Tara, who was in another room with Amira, and they dashed into the bedroom and tumbled onto the bed with us. For the next hour we stayed up past the children's bedtime, snuggled together as a family while Khyber continued to read, with some help from his big sister. Tara and I proudly celebrated the precious time together.

That evening offered one of the most succinct encapsulations of the blessings and the burdens that come out of the work I do to promote literacy and education for young readers in central Asia. It also helped sustain me through the challenges that were to unfold in the weeks ahead.

By February, Sarfraz had come to the conclusion that regardless of how eager we might be to use some of our earthquake-relief money to begin converting our tent schools into permanent structures, circumstances required that we wait. Back in December, we had been able to catch a few flights on the Chinooks, and from above it was easy to see how radically the landscape had been changed. Alluvial fans had been altered, drainage channels had changed, and hillsides that had taken centuries to terrace into arable fields had been eliminated. Thanks to those changes, entire villages would need to relocate, which meant that no one could be sure exactly where hundreds of thousands of people would ultimately end up.

Given this uncertainty, Sarfraz counseled, it was too early to start putting up actual buildings. Instead, he declared, what we needed to concentrate on was figuring out how to provide clean, dependable water sources. In the communities where we were working this was a top priority because, among other reasons, a good source of water is a prerequisite for a school.

In the villages of Baltistan, most of the water systems relied on glacial melt. In the villages of Azad Kashmir, however, there was an almost total reliance on springs, many of which had now been permanently plugged or rerouted. Taking everything into account, Sarfraz thought it was necessary for us to put in small water-collection tanks and delivery pipes for five villages, including Nouseri. With my approval, he paid modest sums to two water engineers to design these systems. He also managed to finagle quite a bit of free PVC piping from the Public Works Department in Rawalpindi, including twenty thousand feet for Nouseri alone.

So far, so good. Who could possibly be opposed to such a project? As it turned out, a Pakistani subcontractor who was working for an American contractor who, in turn, was receiving funding from the USAID objected on the grounds that the Central Asia Institute did not have an official permit to distribute water in Azad Kashmir.

You are an education NGO, he argued, whereas I have pre-